2012 and Beyond
Wisdom Along the Path

The Laws of Attraction & Creation and Other Magnificent Messages from Archangel Metatron

by James Tyberonn

© Copyright 2012 by James Tipton.
All Rights Reserved. No part of this publication may be reproduced, stored in a retrieval system or transmitted in any form or by any means: electronic, mechanical, photocopying, recording or otherwise without written consent.

Cover art © by Daniel B. Holeman – www.AwakenVisions.com

2012 and Beyond: Wisdom Along the Path
by James Tyberonn
ISBN: 978-0-9767035-8-7
Library of Congress Control Number: 2012932074

To order books:
Email: Tyberonn@Earth-Keeper.com,
Website: http://www.Earth-Keeper.com

Ascension, Consciousness Awareness, Mastery, Body Mind Spirit, Energy Science, Source Alignment, Consciousness Expansion, Light, Channeling, Everyday Spirituality, Law of Attraction, Multiimensionality, Consciousness Physics, Life Energy, God, Science & Religion, Spirituality, the Self. Conscious Creation, Angelic Beings, Mayan Calendar, the Pyramids, 12 Wave, Atlantis, Metatron.

STAR QUEST PUBLISHING
RENO, NV   PHOENIX, AZ
New Perspectives in Unified Consciousness.

3030 E. Shangri-La Rd., Phoenix AZ 85028
info@StarQuestPublishing.com 602-482-1568
www.StarQuestPublishing.com/index.htm
Printed in China.

Dedication

This book is dedicated to all on the Path of Knowledge and Wisdom.

From My Heart, James Tyberonn

Contents

The Law of Attraction ~ When and How it Works and Why
it Sometimes Doesn't...6
    Part One ~ The Law of Attraction and Conscious Creation...7
    Part Two ~ Multi-Dimension Influx...........................….......10
    Part Three ~ The Law of Conscious Creation...............…..…..20
The Nature of Light ~ Angelic Beings of Light Realms........37
Our United Nations Experience ~ Metatron Channel at the
United Nations: "The Nation of Humanity"......................…...51
Animal Consciousness ~ The Divinity of Cats and Dogs,
The Sacred Felidae...63
The Mayan Calendar and Time..............…................................84
The Pyramid of the Ascension ~ Awakening of the
12th Wave..................…...110
Doors of Perception..…..............123
Atlantis and Dr Moreau ~ The Metatronic Perspective on
Yeti and Sasquatch...132
Dancing With the Stars..140
The 2012 Express ~ New Earth Demands of 2013.........….....158
About James Tyberonn..185

James Tyberonn

The Law of Attraction ~ When and How it Works and Why it Sometimes Doesn't
Archangel Metatron via James Tyberonn

Greetings Masters! I am Metatron, Lord of Light, and I greet you in a field of Unconditional Love!

Much has been written about the 'Law of Attraction.' We will address this topic herewith, but our sharing separates the Law of Attraction from the Law of Conscious Creation. Indeed, there is a great need to understand the difference.

An essential truth of the Law of Attraction applies to thought. Accordingly, it is imperative you realize that each thought you have has a magnetic frequency. That resonant 'thought-frequency' will attract similar thoughts of like Vibration. The more energy, attention and focus you give that thought, the more powerful it becomes. If you have a fear or worry and dwell on it, a snowball effect can occur in which one fear, one worry draws in another. Likewise, if you think on the positive, those thoughts attract more benevolent vibrations to you. Thoughts evoke feelings of a similar nature. Your auric field will vibrate according to your thoughts.

You attract to yourself that which you fear and that which you love. You must, then, become the dutiful gatekeeper of thought. Each of you must discern and govern where you place your focus.

This is the Law of Attraction. But it is not the end product that allows conscious creation. You are here to learn how to consciously create, but there is much more to the process.

And so we discuss herewith the Law of Attraction, how it works and why it sometimes does not. For it is imperative to understand that there is a difference between unconscious attraction and conscious attraction. There are exceptions, in a manner of speaking, to 'ask and it shall be given.' First there must be belief followed by action, then a harmony of multidimensional 'You.'

Each of you are Multidimensional Beings. In truth, you operate cosmically and terrestrially in many different formats of reality within the eternal 'Now.' Time is a purposed illusion. All of your 'lifetimes' not only occur simultaneously, there is also a constant subconscious communication between your multi-selves. Each lifetime is cocooned in a hologram of the Omni-Earth. Each succinct hologram is a dynamic of chosen realities among infinite probabilities. And accordingly, each 'lifetime' effects the other, and this is an aspect of the Law of Attraction that will be reviewed in this discussion. For it is only in the Mer-Ka-Na State that true conscious creation can occur.

We begin this assay.

Part One ~ The Law of Attraction and Conscious Creation

Dear Ones, you create your reality, and there is no other rule. You are here in the University of Duality to learn how to responsibly create. Now, there are many texts that speak about the concept of how human beings create their perspective realities.

We offer this caveat: it is not thought that on its own is optimally creative, rather it is BELIEF ... belief expressed in thought through conscious 'clear' mind, followed by action.

So to clarify syntax, let us say that in the Law of Attraction, it is wise to substitute the word "Believe" for "Think," because while positive thought can encourage new belief, until you believe what you think you are not generating new reality. Belief generates reality. This is logical.

So understand, beyond the syntax, that thinking positive thoughts can only manifest if they are in sync with your beliefs. For example if, at your core, you BELIEVE you are unworthy of abundance or, in your core mind, believe that the accumulation of abundance is materialistic and therefore wrong, you will not manifest abundance by merely thinking about it. If you believe money is the root of all evil, the LAW of Attraction will not work for you until you change that core belief.

If you believe that you are poor and will always be scraping to make ends meet, then your very belief will create that experience. No matter if you work two or three jobs, your core belief is generated, projected into dimensionality and indeed will be manifested. You will struggle economically.

If you believe you are not 'very smart,' your brain will take on that belief, and you will be limited. If you believe you are not attractive, you will project that image to all around you telepathically.

You constantly project your beliefs, and their manifestations constantly "meet you in the face" when you view the world around you. They form the reflective mirrored- image of your realized beliefs. You cannot escape your beliefs. They are, however, the method by which you create your experience.

In kind, if you believe, in very simple terms, that people mean you well and will treat you kindly, they will. And, if you believe that the world is against you, then so it will be in your experience. And, if you believe that your body will age and begin to weaken at age 40, then it will. Do you catch our 'drift?'

You are in physical existence to learn and understand that your beliefs, energetically translated into feelings, thoughts and emotions, cause all experience. Period. Now, your experience can change your beliefs, and at any time you are in control of what you choose to believe. The key is to form BELIEF through 'oversoul' Mer-Ka-Na aspectual conscious choice and not by unconscious programming.

Now, let's take this concept into multi-dimensionality.

Imagine that you have a number of lifetimes as a monk or priest where you have taken strict poverty vows. You have shunned the 'material' and adhere strongly to the BELIEF that money is 'the root of all evil.'

All lifetimes are simultaneous in the eternal now. In the present lifetime there is the focus on creating your reality. You have need for abundance. You realize money is not evil, it is simply energy and that it can be used for many positive things.

You have read all the books, read all the articles on how positive thinking triggers the 'Law of Attraction,' yet you are still not bringing in abundance. Could it be that you are multidimensionally 'outnumbered?'

If you have a dozen ongoing lifetimes in their NOW moment simultaneously shunning, rejecting what they BELIEVE to be 'material things,' and you have one lifetime trying to create abundance, which effort contains the most energy projection?

You have the ability in NOW mind, in Mer-Ka-Na to change the seeming past and create a unified harmonic of that which you desire and believe. And, Dear Ones, money is not evil! It is energy, and in the new paradigm you are required to learn to create in responsible loving manner. You CAN have what you want, what you need, but the Belief must be harmonic in multi-dimensionality.

It is not as simple as "Ask and it shall be given." It must be projected in clear harmonic mind. And mind is above brain. Mind is multidimensional.

Part Two ~ Multi-Dimension Influx

Now, the multidimensional aspect of human experience is quintessential to your understanding of the mechanics of the 'Law of Attraction.'

A key part of understanding your multidimensionality is that your higher self, the part of you above physicality, scripted certain of your 'life growth challenges' ... and that these cannot be avoided or wished away. Rather, they are 'required' courses in the curriculum of the 'University of Earth' that you yourself have chosen to complete for higher good. And you can't skip the classes.

They will come to you because you enrolled. They are a part of the 'Law of Attraction' from higher mind and cannot be repelled.

This, then, is an area in which duality thinking, of trying to wish away a seeming obstacle, seems to defy the 'Law of Attraction.' You may find yourself in an uncomfortable scenario at work, find that all the 'positive thinking' applications seem to fall flat. That is because there is a lesson here that must be faced, and until it is faced, it will repeat over and over again until it is completed ... because you have attracted it to you from higher mind, and duality-aspect brain is unable to avoid it. It is only completed when you master it.

Accepting the Challenge

While it is true that your thoughts and beliefs create the reality you experience in duality, you in higher aspect thoughtfully and carefully compose and create the challenges that you face. These have great purpose. Whether you truly believe it or not, you write your own tests. So while 'positive thinking' is a key frequency, positive thinking is meant to help you approach your life lessons and does not circumvent the learning process itself. You cannot just ignore or wish away the growth lessons you script for yourself in order to expand. That is because your chosen setups are in most cases outside, beyond the ability of the duality aspect of ego-brain to remove or will away. You will face them, because you have, in divine self, willed it from higher perspective. In higher mind you have scripted your challenges.

We assure you that there is nothing more stimulating, more worthy of actualization than your manifested desire to evolve, to change for the better. That is indeed each of your lifetime missions. It is not enough to meditate or to visualize the desired goal being accomplished if you do not act upon the inner voice, the drive from which your meditations and visualizations arise.

Intent, focus and meditation must absolutely be teamed with action. Becoming impeccable and eventually achieving your enlightenment does not mean, as some religions indirectly imply, that you are suddenly in a blissful state of oblivion or in some distant state of nirvana. Masters, we tell you that you are as much a part of a nirvana now as you ever will be, you simply need to discover it within you.

There will indeed be cycles within your emotional state; that is part of being human. There will be times in which you feel apathetic and depressed. Not only the problems you face but even certain astronomical gravities can be the source of such despair on their own. All of these must be faced, and can be surmounted.

So be aware that 'Nirvana,' in your vernacular, is achieved attitudinally, not through avoidance, ignorance or escape but through impeccable confrontation of the reality projection that surrounds you. Earth experience, duality mastery is difficult. This is a great truth, one of the greatest truths of duality and one commonly misunderstood. The study and mastery of life requires work. You cannot simply put the text book under your pillow and sleep on it. It must be read and understood a page at a time, moment by moment.

So, then, your full understanding and accepting that your life is a construction of 'setups' that you planned in order to enable your spiritual growth is an even greater truth. You see, when you accept this noble truth, you have the opportunity to transcend it.

That which you term 'destiny' is in truth the situations you preplanned for your life lesson. And, Dear Ones, that very self scripted 'destiny,' in your terms, will assist you to both face your challenges and then manifest your desires but not because you protest what you do not like. In order to experience the light of your desire, you must ignite the passion that will free it from the stronghold where it has been closely guarded. The greatest path is to accept the challenge of self purification by being a living example of your own light rather than protesting the darkness that still exists within the world in 3-D or choosing to insulate yourself from it.

Acceptance

Masters, by accepting that you are here to face challenges, then you can more robustly create the energy needed to face them.

Because once it is accepted, the fact that life can be difficult no longer scares you, rather it motivates the spiritual warrior into resolve.

The greatest issue you have in accepting ultimate ownership and responsibility for your actions lies in the core desire to avoid the pain of the consequences of that behavior. But we tell you that it is the confrontational courage of impeccably solving problems that provides and indeed nurtures meaningful growth in your life.

Facing your problems is the serendipitous cutting edge that distinguishes between success and failure or, better said, between growth and stagnation. Problems call forth your best effort to resolve and refine courage and wisdom within the impeccable seeker.

It is categorically because of stressful predicaments and obstructions that you grow mentally and spiritually. It is through the pain of confronting and resolving life puzzles and 'setups' that you learn the greater meaning of the science of love. Dear Hearts, the candid fact is that some of your most poignant accomplishments and indeed greatest growths are spawned when you are placed in the troubling crossroads of conundrum.

Your greatest trials and revelations take place in times when you are outside of your 'comfort zone', feeling bewildered, unfulfilled, or even in a state of agonizing despair. For it is in such moments, propelled by your discomfort, that you are compelled to burst out of the confining cages and seek a better, more spiritually satisfying way of life.

Impeccability ~ The State of Grace

What, then, is impeccability? We are not understating the base premise when we define impeccability simply as **'always trying** *your best.'* To remain impeccable requires more effort as the scope of your gained wisdom and consciousness expands. The greater your consciousness, the more you 'know.' The more you know, the greater the responsibility to live accordingly.

You are in the process of expanding your vibratory awareness, of becoming a conscious participant with the soul. You are becoming what your soul is, discovering your greater identity. Dear Ones, when you grow spiritually, it is because you have opened to seek growth and are taking action, working to achieve it.

Impeccability involves the deliberate extension of your Beingness into evolution. Impeccability puts you in the state of grace. Impeccability does not infer that you have achieved enlightenment or have learned all you need to learn. Rather it means that you are on the only track, the right pathway to get there.

So we will define Impeccability in two layers, two phase formats:

1. **Conditional Impeccability**: *This is when the entity is not highly advanced yet working toward Mastery. Doing one's best. Utilizing knowledge to the best of one's ability to do the right thing, even when there may be ignorance and innocent misconceptions. By that we mean you truly believe what you are doing is the right course, even if it is not the full or expansive truth. All of you go through such phases. In this phase if you make a mistake, it is an honest mistake in which you genuinely believed you were doing what you felt is right.*
2. **Mastery Impeccability**: *This is the phase of the soul in human existence that is on the cusp of Mastery. One highly advanced and walking the talk. Having no inner conflict between what one believes to be the right path and what one actuates.*

Both phases activate that which you may term as an accelerated state of grace. Grace is assistance from the Divine Self to help the outcome of situations when one is trying their best. It may be thought of as the 'Guardian Angel,' because in many cases that is exactly what a Guardian Angel is, your Divine Self serendipitously intervening in situations to assist you on your path.

If we were to redefine what your religious texts consider as sin, it would not be in terms of the commandments, rather it would be: "knowledge not utilized." Taking actions you know to be incorrect, actions in conflict to your highest beliefs.

Wisdom Is Within

All of you desire wisdom greater than your own. Seek and you will find, and, Masters, you can find it 'hidden' inside you. And, sadly, that is often the last place you look. It takes work. You see, the divine interface between God and man is within that which your academics term as the subconscious.

Even your religious texts tell you that God is within you, that you are a spark of the Divine. The subconscious mind or 'back brain,' in your terms, is the part of you that is God. The portion of your greater self that contains the knowledge of 'All That Is,' the part of you that contains the Akashic Records, the soul memory of everything.

Since the subconscious is the Divine Mind within you, the goal of spiritual growth is achieved by entering into that sacred 'Garden of Wisdom.' It is entered by quieting the ego-mind. Meditation has ever been the gateway. It is the key to quieting the personality-ego narration and allowing the 'Voice of the Divine Soul' to be heard. We say again, effort is required. There are no short cuts.

James Tyberonn

The reattainment of God-ness is the purpose of your individual existence on the polarity plane. You are born that you might become, as a conscious individual, a physical expression of God. A divine expression in Beingness.

The challenge is your soul quest, your true purpose, and in physical sojourns the clock is ever ticking. Obtaining Godhood in physicality is achieved on time release, through immaculate desire that is actuated in the physical realm by merging with the wisdom of the non physical. Time matters.

In polarity, the current shifting of paradigms and energies can throw you off center rather easily in these quickening times. Your true purpose is often difficult to subjectively define, and your understanding and ballast lies juxtaposed between illusion and perceived reality. You may feel you are living in a distortion and that nothing is exactly as it seems. In the process, you can become confused and complacent. You can lose track of time.

Dear Ones, your lives, each moment of your physical life is precious, far more so than some of you realize. Far more than most of you utilize. Time is a precious commodity, and it is finite within your duality. Each of you reading these words will at some point in the future transition out of the physical. In your vernacular, you will experience death, you will die. This is a condition of physicality as you know it. Yet, so many of you act as though you will live forever. Indeed, the soul is eternal, but you will not ever be the same person, the same personality or expression that you are now, in any lifetime or in any other aspect of your 'Beingness.'

You are here to learn, Dear Ones, you are here to learn the expressions of your own Godliness within duality, and indeed duality is a gift. Life is a gift. You are here to learn how to cocreate, for indeed you are cocreators of the Universe, of the Cosmos. You are here to achieve Mastery, and so many of you are very close, very near that achievement.*

Seize the Day

Masters, until you truly value yourself, you will not be in the grace of impeccability and thus not be motivated to truly value and optimize your time. Unless you place great value on your allotted time, you will not do your 'best' with it. "Carpe Diem" is translated as "Seize the Day," and this is so appropriate.

You must seize each moment! So many of you, despite your good intentions, allow yourselves to be tranquilized into complacency during certain phases or within certain conditions of your chosen sojourns. Many of you waste time; misuse time, and lifetime after lifetime can be squandered. That which you do not face, that which you do not resolve in any one moment or lifetime will resurface. You will repeat the setup until you successfully solve it, and that is indeed a great truth.

Masters, utilizing your time in duality is quintessential, and that is a complex undertaking, for it necessitates that you seek impeccability. It requisites love of self, for until you genuinely value yourself, you truly do not value your life and time. And until you value your time, you will not be compelled to maximize how you spend it.

It is natural Discipline that is the basic set of tools to solve life problems. Without discipline it is difficult for you to have the driver required to focus on the work of solving your problems. Simply stated, you can become immobilized ... apathetic, complacent or lazy. On the 'Ladder of Ascension,' you are either moving up, sitting still or moving down.

In third dimensional physics, there is a law that states that energy which is highly organized will naturally degrade when not in dynamic state. It is easier by natural law to be in a state of complacency in the physical plane than to be in an upwardly mobile condition. That is clearly logical. It is the Law of Love that motivates all souls into greater consciousness, and that requires dynamics ... work! Laziness is in a real sense one of your biggest obstacles, because work means swimming against the tide. Seize the Day!

Perfect Order

Some of you say and feel that, "Everything works out as it should, all is in perfect order." But, Masters, that concept is something of a paradox, and, like a face card, it is upside down either way you look at it. Do you understand?

From the higher perspective, all is in perfect order, but from the perspective of humankind within duality, it is not! If it were, there would be no need for lessons, no need for that which you term reincarnation.

One need but take a look around to know that the plight of humankind on the planet Earth is far from being perfect. Indeed, it will NOT work out as it should until you make it so!

Unresolved Energy Blockage

Masters, on the final walk of Mastery, most of your major issues have been dealt with, and we honor you for that. What remains may, however, be elusive to confront. And it is important to confront any and all unresolved issues and energies.

We say this without judgment. We point this out in order to assist you. For, in time, all must be dealt with. The more advanced you become, the more difficult it can be to sweep up the last remaining bits of unresolved issues, because they are often well hidden. The unresolved energy, the final issues can become polarized and repelled outside your mental field, forgotten in the residues of many lifetimes. Dear Hearts, take time to self review in multidimensional, Mer-Ka-Na aspect. Please determine what is left to be worked on.

Polarity Physics ~ The 'Law of Opposite Attraction'

Masters, the closer you get to light, the stronger you attract the dark. Light attracts bugs! The more you advance, the more criticism you will draw, and that requires wisdom to deal with.

The polarity aspect of the 'Law of Opposite Attraction' herewith comes into play. From a state of detachment, what takes place is electromagnetics. Pure positive energy has the greatest 'magnetic' attraction to negative energy. So as your light shines brighter, the magnetic to polar opposite increases. It can be managed, but you must have the light, humility, strength and discipline to deflect it.

So dealing with affronts, the hard energy of jealousy, hatred and anger are an important piece of the puzzle in achieving the Master level of Impeccability. How do you deal with this? Don't take anything personally is perhaps easier said than done, but it is quite true. Your bible talks of turning the other cheek. But this does not mean that you apologize when someone steps on your foot. Part of the paradox is indeed standing up for your truth. But it does mean that you do not step on the feet of others, intentionally or otherwise. Do you understand?

Standing in your truth is peaceful action. It is a benevolent expression of aggression that allows grace and dignity to be retained on both sides of any conflict or attack. It sends the attacking energy back to its source but without malice and with love.

Each of you has an opportunity to stand in impeccability within any conflict. You can deal with conflict without engaging it. Do you understand? Deal with, face it from a stance of emotional detachment, as the observer, and that is not easy, yet it is the way of the Master. It is how you 'don't take anything personally,' you detach from the emotional reaction.

Each of you has an opportunity to be impeccable every day. The scenario in which you recognize your own failings, your own conflict with integrity is the day you encompass Mastery level Impeccability, and indeed it is a journey. Likewise, the day you stand in your truth with willingness to recognize another person's truth, you encompass integrity.

The divine mind is only achieved, only accessed through crystalline Mer-Ka-Na resonance, within crystalline thought waves. Crystalline thought is above emotion, above petty feelings. It is achieved in detachment. It is the crystalline lake of Shamballa, of true Nirvana, as smooth as glass, no waves distorting its mirrored visage.

Part 3 ~ The Law of Conscious Creation

Greetings Masters! Dear Ones, there is the science behind the Law of Attraction, and that science is the Law of Belief. The Law of Belief governs what you create in your lives. Within the Law of Belief are the addendums of the life 'setups' you plan and contract to yourself for growth. But the lessons you arrange are met through your confrontation and disciplined effort.

It is therefore essential that you fully realize that you are never at the mercy of events, you are not helplessly fated to face the unexplainable like a ship lost at sea. Masters, neither psychological events nor physical events have control over you. When you humans fully comprehend the vast capacity of your brain to hold a diversity of conclusive beliefs associated with your experiences, you will see that you have an infinite array of choices.

But for those of you stuck in old patterns and limiting beliefs, you are mired in a repetitive cycle of predetermined responses, including the propensity to block new solutions through denial of better thinking. In that sense if you do not learn from past errors, you are self fated to repeat them. Indeed, you will repeat the cycle until you learn how the process of achieving Divine Mind functions. That is true for all humans. You must challenge yourself to break free.

Three Laws

There are three separately governed processes under the Law of Attraction. The three have succinctly different criteria for achievement. Let us define the primary aspect of each Law:

- *The Law of Attraction: Thoughts have a frequency and attract like frequencies*
- *The Law of Belief: Knowing beyond doubt. You can only manifest what you believe is possible*
- *The Law of Conscious Creation: The conscious ability to focally manifest objectives and events via Mer-multidimensional mind in Mer-Ka-Na*

Soul Contract Setups

And so we again stress emphatically that it is your beliefs that are projected to form your individual and group reality. As we have discussed in the previous messages on this topic, there are scenarios planned by your higher self, your Divine Mind aspect, that may be termed 'set-ups' or soul contracts that you yourself have chosen as growth lessons to assist you in moving into greater wisdom.

With that reminder in hand, we also tell you that 'karma,' in your terms, is not a debt owed to one from another, in the higher sense. Rather it is ever to the Self, it is balancing the Divine Self.

Let us also assert that if you have a goal or objective in 3-D that would conflict with higher self, then it will not in most cases be manifest unless it is chosen as a growth lesson. For example, if a human desires wealth, and that wealth would either be misused or would stop the growth process, then the higher self may reject such a desire from manifesting. In some cases, humans who have all of their 3-D material 'needs' met are less compelled to search for expansion.

Dear Ones, when you find yourself within the confines of any experience that is uncomfortable or not to your liking, you must understand that YOU created that seeming conundrum. Within this axiom, there are indeed, within duality, scenarios in linear time that you must face. Whether one accepts it or not, every circumstance and every resulting action, however dire, was absolutely self created.

If, for example in an extreme circumstance, a crime is actually committed and an individual is duly sentenced to prison, those actions will be faced and experienced. The sentenced prisoner cannot, in most duality circumstances, simply wish it away. Rather, they must face the duality they have themselves created in linear time. There are Laws of Cause and Effect in 3-D that will play themselves out.

Responsibility for not only your actions but, indeed, for your beliefs is a key part of your growing process on the planet of lesson. Owning both is essential. But by facing them, you can change the landscape around you.

Dear Human, you must understand that whenever you seek to avoid the responsibility for your own actions, you generally do so by attempting to give that responsibility, the 'blame' to some other individual, group or cause. But in that process of shifting blame, you unconsciously give away your power and take away the ownership that allows you to 're-create.'

In kind, as we have already explained in the second segment of this discussion, the difficulty most of you have in accepting self responsibility for your behavior lies in the desire to avoid the pain and guilt of the consequences of the very actions that resulted. You don't like to admit your errors.

But in less obvious circumstances of abundance – lack and untoward relationships – you must not only change the nature of your conscious thoughts but also the belief in those very expectations ... and then act on those beliefs.

Unconscious Programming

You create your own reality from what you choose to believe about yourselves and the world around you. Period. If you do not deliberately and consciously choose your own beliefs, you are unconsciously programmed. You will mindlessly absorb them from your 3-D culture, schooling and surroundings. If you are accountable and responsible for your actions, how can you afford NOT to question your beliefs? How you define yourself and the world around you forms your belief which, in turn, forms your reality.

Once you fully comprehend that your beliefs form reality, then and only then are you no longer a captive to the events you experience. You simply have to learn the mechanics and methods. It is only when you believe, and program that belief to fully override and replace previous erroneous beliefs, that the integral field of the triad of the 3 step function of Own, Change, Action is completed. In the process, thoughts must harmonize with beliefs and be followed by ACTION!

So we devote the remainder of this discourse to conscious creation. Keeping in mind that you are advanced on the path in order to consciously create.

You Are Not at the Mercy of Circumstance

You are NOT at the mercy of your circumstances, but that belief is, interestingly, the reason you erroneously think you are. Take a moment to consider that. It is the Law of Belief.

If you believe that circumstances have you trapped, then they do, and they will until you change that core belief. You are creators learning how to cocreate. You are here to learn that you can and do create. One of your key reasons for being in duality Earth is to learn how to create responsibly and consciously. The principle professor is often Dr. Cause and Effect, and this doctor makes house calls!

You reap what you sow, and however uncomfortable, the untoward harvest is the very means for consideration of what got you there. To break out of circumstances that are caused by our psychology requires conscious disciplined effort for change to occur.

The key, again, is your belief. There is little difference if you believe that your present life is caused by incidents in your early childhood or by past lives over which you equally feel you have no control. Your events, your lives, your experiences are caused by your present beliefs. Change the present beliefs and your life changes, not only in the present but in the past and future in kind. That is the creative power of belief.

Masters, irregardless of your level of Light Quotient, whether you are unconsciously creating or consciously manifesting, you cannot escape your beliefs. They are the enzymes through which you create your experience.

Processes of Brain and Mind

Masters, the reason that most of the books and commercialized teachings on manifestation do not work is because they do not have the understanding of deeper mind versus 3-D brain. Most are about manifesting monetary wealth, and in most cases, the only one truly manifesting is the publisher from book sales.

There are many nuances, many aspects unexplained in the texts. Even when you expand the mind, you must optimize and balance the auric field for the Crystalline aspect that allows creation to function.

The Key Evolvement Principles for Accessing the Law of Creation are:

1. *Expanded Programming of the Brain – Knowledge into Belief*
2. *Release of Ego-Personality Control to Divine-Mind Aspect of Higher Consciousness*
3. *Maintain EMF Balance*
4. *Activate the Mer-Ka-Na Crystalline aspect of Pituitary, Pineal, and Thymus*
5. *Maintain Balance and Clarity*

It is essential you understand that the 3-D brain, the ego-personality aspect incorporated in your physical 3-D biology is programmed for 'survival' in a primary coding. It is the 'survival' code that brings in the warning signals which involve cautions often experienced as fear and doubt. The frontal mind, the ego-personality aspect is engineered to dominate your 3-D consciousness in order to allow linear time flow and survival within the physical plane. The challenge is that in order to arise above 3-D consciousness, you must rise out of ego consciousness and flow into Divine Mind within the Seat of the Soul, the gateway into Divine Mind.

The brain is in 3-D, the mind is of higher dimension, and within higher mind is your Divinity. The brain operates in 3-D, and, in a manner of speaking, its 3-D programming is somewhat dominant in the field of duality. It operates in a more confined paradigm, and in order to to expand into mind, you must operate 'outside the box' to engage your true creativity.

Clarity in Your Objectives

The significance of defined clarity is important in creation. You humans only partially engage your wishes through 'Someday I will' dreamscapes. That is like partially programming a computer program. Is it any surprise that it does not happen?

Someday I will travel, one day I will be rich, some day I will realize my dreams ... these, then, become merely 'maybes' spaced in a distance. So what you are attempting to create always stays at the distance, the someday you programmed. You did not put it into the present. Yes, the dream is the first part, but it must be clear, concise and followed by definite actions.

Your brain has two hemispheres, one dealing with intellect, one with feeling. The brain works through biochemical activations and stimulus. The intensity and clarity of a thought program is extremely important for it to become a belief.

You see, your brain is a 3-D living computer. It must be dealt with in defined terms. It will not work with 'maybe' or 'can I?'

For example, if one were taken into a deep hypnotic state and asked, "Can the mind heal the dis-ease in this body?" The answer would be "Yes." But it is the empirical answer to whether it is possible for the mind to heal the body. It is not the healing.

The Noble Path

Every thought produces a biochemical enzyme. That enzyme works with the physical and nonphysical in sync with the programming. One of the exceptions to the concept of 'Ask and it Shall be given' is that unless the asking is channeled from within, in sync with higher mind, it may have little effect.

So a human on the path in a relatively advanced state of consciousness may well neutralize from a higher stance desires that would impede progress. There is, then, a natural filtering for those in a state of grace. Goals must be worthy.

The most noble goal is to learn the mysteries of life, to gain wisdom and Mastery. But to achieve these goals, you will have to take on certain pressures and stresses that are taxing. It requires discipline and will.

If you are lazy, you will not get there. You must take on the task to achieve it. Therefore attempts to create a challenge-free life may be in stark conflict with a life intent on learning. Goals have challenges. Masters do not plan challenge-free lifetimes.

Mind Is The Builder

Mind is the builder, and focused will power is the activator. The more responsibility you appropriately take on, the more your frequency will increase.

Learning to program the brain is essential. The brain is a biological computer with 3-D filters and 3-D programs that are ingrained from birth. Unless you were born in a Tibetan monastery, your programming has come from what we will term socio-cultural indoctrinations. Most social programming teaches you to accept a very limited view of human existence and human ability. You are taught to believe only what you can sensually detect through sight, hearing, taste, smell or touch.

Dear Ones, know that the physical world of matter you see around you is imagery that you sensually interpret and project. It is received in the eye and transferred via the optic nerve to the brain. What is received stimulates neurons, and a response occurs through a biochemical reaction that is thermal in nature.

Because you generally believe what you see, smell, taste or hear you accept it, you believe it as real. You then decide if it is pleasing or not. The brain then releases neurons based on like or dislike. This is how your reality and attraction works. You are initially attracted to people who are attractive, have a melodious voice and smell good! Your physical sensual body says yes or no.

In kind, the brain takes ideas and either accepts them or deflects them according to program parameters. In truth, the brain is unable to differentiate between an actual event or a psychological one, such as a dream. In multidimensional mind the two are the same.

And although the human brain is capable of receiving information and frequencies from well above 3-D, most humans program it to reject anything above 3-D frequencies of sensory conformity. The brain computer thus receives only what you allow it to receive.

In such limiting archetypical programming, the only parts of your brain that are activated are the right and left hemispheres of the upper cerebrum and portions of the lower cerebellum, composing and imposing an activity level of only about 10-12 percent of the brain. The brain activity and processes in the neocortex of the cerebral hemispheres conduct the primary activity in the physical realm.

The 90 percent majority of your brain remains unused, unactivated, programmed into dormancy. That is because any thought that does not fit in with the limited thinking programs of your cultural programming or dogma, you auto-deflect.

Expanding Your Belief Horizons

Herein is one of the great reasons the 'Law of Attraction' does not work for you: limited belief from limited thinking programs. To be so narrow-minded is to be closed to the grand possibility of anything existing beyond the small band of frequency that can be perceived through the five senses of your physical 3-D body.

So how do you expand the brain? How do you open to mind? How do you reprogram the computer?

The answer is simple but seemingly a difficult hurdle for many of you to accomplish. It is by doing. It is by examination and study and by willing self to open.

Accordingly, the very desire to expand attracts powerful thought frequencies that will allow for expansion. And then every occasion in which you openly accept an idea that is beyond your accepted parameters, that idea activates yet another part of your brain into purposeful use.

Each time you do that, the expansive idea will offer itself as a carrier to expand your field of belief and will allow greater Cosmic reasoning. That process sincerely repeated will attract new ideas with study and meditation. In kind, this cycle will activate other portions of your brain for more expansion, new programming and new reception by accepting in clear mind Mer-Ka-Na.

When you have no doubt, when you know and it is absolute ... it is Belief. It is through expanded mind that you begin the steps of creating your destiny.

How do you functionally expand the brain and open the doors to Divine Mind? It is not done in one illuminating flash realization. It is not a one step Divine Anointing. The sacred pathway to that which you may term 'Enlightenment' is achieved in deliberate steps.

There are many in metaphysics that want to open the book of knowledge and skip over to the final chapter. It does not work that way.

It begins by self exploration, by carefully auditing what works and does not work for you. In this method you allow fresh and expansive ideas to enter the brain from the Divine Mind as high frequency thought. Then you process and contemplate it, experience the new concept by embracing it, acting it out. Evolve it and drive it with emotion, and live the new information into knowledge and wisdom.

The Static in the Field

The issue most humans have in not changing their beliefs is blind acceptance of mental 3-D programming. You can think positive thoughts, think positive change, but if in your deeper mind you doubt they will occur, then they will not.

Doubt is one blockage that prevents manifestation of your desires. If you doubt, you do not believe. Doubt in the brain creates a biochemical reaction. It activates a neuron carrier in the brain that flows from the Pituitary gland to the Pineal and blocks the 'gateway' from opening. The doubt is there because you do not believe.

As we have mentioned, the survival aspect programming of the Personality-Ego brain utilizes 'fear' in duality as a warning system. However, the duality aspect, the double edge of that sword is that fear out of context can reach into many negative emotions including depression, doubt, hatred, jealousy and self contempt. These are, at their root, negative aspects of fear, and fear creates static in the auric field and can lead to auric bleeding. As taught in the Metatronic Keys, the human Aura must be integral to amplify into Mer-Ka-Na. A fissured or disrupted energy field is unable to optimally operate in the Law of Creation.

Biochemical Process

The belief thought-images that surround you are cocreated in mass fields by all of humanity in agreement in the macro. Individually they are projected according to your light quotient. These manifest into physical reality.

This involves a physical process. Thought frequencies are digitally received and are immediately propelled biochemically within the brain.

Mental enzymes are connected with the Pineal gland. The Pineal gland receives them as geo-coded transmissions. Each image, each thought is being interpreted and sorted according to its energetic signature. They must pass through the program parameter of belief after reception at the Pineal. Your brain screens what is determined as real or unreal, believable or unbelievable according to the Light Quotient programmed into the brain. The biochemicals generated are produced with acceptance ingredient or rejection ingredient. These are allowed to open or close the gate to higher mind accordingly.

These biochemicals are sent as coded neurons and are the delivery mechanism of this thought-energy. They contain all the codified data necessary for translating, or not, any thought or image into physical actuality.

Thoughts which are congruent with belief move to reproduce the inner image within the brain and through each nerve fiber of the body physical. These, then, are the initial fires of gestation for forming the new reality.

The next step is through clear mind intent, the force of will, will driven by the acceleration of emotion and feeling. This done, the physical body releases the objective in a digital code to the sublime body, the intact Auric Field in a semisolid, congealed light code, projected and accelerated from the chakric system.

The Aura must be intact and optimal in 13-20-33 cycle and reach. It then passes through the Mer-Ki-Va to Mer-Ka-Va to Mer-Ka-Na field. All propelled by will. The clarity and intensity you insert behind the thought-desire or goal determines to a great degree the immediacy of its materialization. Once you learn the mechanics of conscious creation, it is essential, then, to utilize the engine of genuine desire with image visualization and emotion to complete the process of physical manifestation.

The Law of Conscious Creation

There is no physical object about you nor any experience in your life that you have not created. This includes your physical form, your body. Masters, there is nothing about your own physical image that you have not made. In fact, if you were able to view self in other life sojourns, you would be surprised at how many similar physical characteristics you create in that which would be termed sequential lifetimes.

When you have Divine Wisdom, you can create kingdoms unlimited. When you have knowledge, there is nothing to fear, for then there is no thing, no element, no principality, no understanding that can ever threaten or enslave or intimidate you. When fear is given knowledge, it is called Enlightenment.

You have a natural rhythm of existing in the physical and nonphysical. It is your waking and sleep states. Dreams are one of your greatest natural therapies and assist as connectors between the interior and exterior realities and universes. Your normal consciousness benefits by excursions and rest in those other fields of nonphysical actuality that are entered when you sleep, and the so-called sleeping consciousness will also benefit by frequent excursions into the physical matter waking state.

But let us tell you that the imagery you see in both is at its base mental interpretations of digital frequential fields of core consciousness units. The frequency which your brain receives is actually a digital code, a crystalline pattern of symbols (akin to that which you may term as X's and O's), which you interpret and translate into images and feelings.

It is not so difficult for you to accept that you create your dreams as it is to accept that you also create your physical reality, but you do both. You also determine if both or either are real ... or not.

Reemphasizing the Blockage of Doubt

The issue most humans have in not changing their beliefs is blind acceptance of mental 3-D programming. You can think positive thoughts, think positive change, but if in your deeper mind you doubt they will occur, then they will not.

So we return to programming and its effect on manifestation within the Law of Attraction. Doubt is one blockage that prevents manifestation of your desires. If you doubt, you do not believe. Doubt in the brain creates a biochemical reaction. It activates a neuron carrier in the brain that flows from the Pituitary gland to the Pineal and blocks the 'gateway' from opening. The doubt is there because you do not believe.

The Pineal

Through the ages it has been known that the Pineal is the interface between the higher dimensions and the physical realm. It can be said, then, to be the gateway between the ego-personality, brain and the Divine Mind. It has been termed by metaphysicians such as Descartes and Edgar Cayce as being the 'Seat of the Soul.'

The Pineal is the agent of advancing knowing into reality manifestation. The Pineal works with the Pituitary to open the bridge, the gateway between the physical and nonphysical, between brain and mind. Whatever knowledge you allow yourself to believe can only become a reality by the Pineal first opening the gate to the Divine. It does this by interpreting the frequency of thought into a thermal biochemical electrical current throughout your body and opening to mind.

Your human brain transforms the thoughts you generate into thousands of biochemicals every second. Not every thought of the ordinary brain reaches into Higher Mind, as we have explained.

Divine Mind

Divine Wisdom comes from Divine Mind, and when you allow mind to take the reins over ego-personality, you achieve the wisdom of Divine Creativity. It is this wisdom distilled from knowledge that gives you the ability to enter the Law of Creation. Once entered, then know what you want to create and take action toward it.

The human body is an instrument that can be used to access the amazing and extraordinary energies of the Divine. But there are dedicated principles for accessing the Divine. When the body is fine tuned, wisdom is achieved, the aura is maintained in balance to achieve Mer-Ka-Na, and the doors to the Law of Creation through the Law of Belief and Attraction are opened.

For that to occur, all systems must work in balanced synchronicity. If you use your body for physical gratification rather than as an instrument to achieve the Divine ... you will reap what you sow.

Closing

You are ever the Master of each experience. Even in your most abandoned states of seeming helplessness, you are the scripter of each iota of that experience. Yet if you will utilize determination and wisdom by owning the responsibility to reflect upon your situation and to search diligently for the Law upon which being is established, you then become the wise Master, directing your energies with intelligence, and fashioning thoughts to worthy focus and realization.

One thought attracts another. Positive energy attracts more positive energy. One intelligent thought attracts another. Likewise, when you dwell in self pity, depression and issues of poor self esteem, you draw more of these to you. That is the Law of Attraction.

Such is the conscious human, the Master, and you can only thus evolve by discovering within Self the Laws of Conscious Creating; the discovery of which is totally a regulated science. It is a matter of application, self analysis and experience.

Masters, as has been said, you are powerful spiritual beings having a human experience. You are truly magnificent Beings of Power, Intelligence and Love. When you discover that, you become the manager of your own thoughts, and you thus have the key to every situation. In Mer-Ka-Na, you are optimizing the Law of Attraction, Law of Belief and Law of Creation, which are the abilities of the Divine within each of YOU, the transforming and regenerative agencies by which you may make what you will.

You can indeed intentionally manifest your world and in doing so experience what is termed the Kingdom of Heaven. Conscious Creation is your destiny, and you can all make your lives the golden experience you responsibly desire.

I am Metatron, and I share with you these Truths. You are Beloved.

And so it is ... and it is so. AA Metatron via James Tyberonn

The Nature of Light ~ Angelic Beings of Light Realms
Archangel Metatron via James Tyberonn

Greetings! I am Metatron, Lord of Light! As the heralded 2012 approaches, we encompass each of you in a vector and field of Unconditional Love within coded light. We nurture you, we honor each of you. We know you by heart, by tone, by name. It has always been so!

You are entering 2012, the 12th Wave of the Ascension ... and so much awaits you. The anticipation is palpable, in both your physical realm and ours. Oh Dear Human, can you feel it?!

The entry of 2012 will be quite different than your typical January for many on the planet. Rather than an energetic decline that often occurs after your holiday season, there will not be the 'January doldrum blues.' Rather a quickening, an excitement, a crisp energy that will sharpen immensely after the new moon of January 23, 2012.

And so we speak on the nature of Light and of the Angelic Beings of Light. *And we tell you in emphatic sincerity that you are all, at source, amazing Beings of Divine Light. Angels are indeed, among you. Although humanity are a different expression of life than the Light Beings of the Angelic Realm, when a human ascends, the energy projection is harmonically attuned with the Angelic Resonance, and Angels are frequencially attracted to you.*

Guardian Angels

Those whom you term Guardian Angels are in truth a unique melding of an aspect of your higher self with the Divine. A succinct energy field that may be termed a 'thought form' is created and energetically fed and filtered by your individual soul in conjunction with Angelic Forces in primary format. This field of 'Guardianship' can be expressed in myriad partnerships. These partnerships can include members of your 'soul group' both in and above the physical realm. Angelics and 'deities' that you pray to intermesh with your higher self to form a unique 3rd energy, both part of you and of the 'Angelic,' but with a somewhat separate identity. For example, if you pray to Ganesh or to Saint Germain or to an Archangel, that energy field becomes a 'personalized' guardian partner. This energy is also quite capable of interacting with you in the form of a 'Totem' or through a household pet.

Symbiotic Levels of Hierarchy

I, Metatron exist on two separate but symbiotic levels. The most familiar and accessible to humanity is as Archangel Metatron, yet on the higher level I exist as Metatron, Lord of Light. But even this analogy cannot encompass or define my nature and is only capable of doing so in aspectual terms.

As 'Lord of Light,' I am a generator of the base units of realities and universes. This level is devoid of that which you would term personality. It is analogous to an engine, a divine conscious computer of energy intensities beyond the gamma, illumination unimaginable to you. And there are levels well beyond me. As Archangel Metatron, I nurture life.

I communicate with the channel, Tyberonn, not in words but in light code 'packets.' He receives this communication by pre-earth agreement, a 'contract,' if you will, of service for these times. In higher aspect, Tyberonn is originally Pleiadean and a member of the Cosmic Council of Light. We have had service together in other sojourns and dimensions. These codes are emitted from my higher aspect, transduced on the Archangelic *level and received in his higher self intact for interpretation and transcription.*

It can be said that, on the higher aspect, I contain the plurality source, generate and emit the geometric frequencial consciousness codes of all that are transduced into the Angelic Realm of Light. As such, there are both hierarchal and non hierarchal aspects of the Angelic Realm that are self determined by conscious crysto-light and light physics. It can be said that the Light Beings of the Angelic Realm, in Metatronic terms, are conscious units of 'Source Divine Thought' and Beyond-Thought that create Light and 'Beyond-Light.'

The Angelics of the Metatronic Realm generate and embellish Coded-Light. Such light intermelds matter, antimatter, time and space. This is obviously not a conceptual view of Angelic function that is held by the masses of humanity and is much less understood. However, in this context lies the glue that irrevocably adheres the sacred scientific to the sacred spiritual aspect of reality that forms the integral unified circle, key to humanity's evolving beyond duality.

Indeed, in the present era of Ascension you are evolving in ability to absorb greater light, and light is TRUTH, Universal Cosmic Truth of All That Is. The enigma that has obstructed full unity of humanity's consciousness in duality, especially in your present, is that science has omitted the sacred, and the spiritual has excluded the scientific.

It may then surprise some of you to know that there are Hierarchies of Angelics dedicated in functional purpose to those whom you may term as Keepers of Physics. In that role, we are conscious constructs of the 'Laws of Physics' that enable dimensional realities. And we realize that the idea of angels being scientists and engineers will confuse most of you. We are smiling!

James Tyberonn

We tell you that the new metaphysicians, the new Lightworkers and Earth-Keepers, in your vernacular, are the scientists. Indeed, those whom you refer to as the 'Crystal Children' are the 'sacred-savant' scientists that will in the next generations complete the circle of understanding and join the spiritual with the scientific. They will not be religious in the traditional sense, but we tell you that humanity will come closer to understanding 'God' through science than through religion. It is the missing piece of the puzzle.

Ascended Masters

Throughout the eons, humanity has tended to consider Ascended Masters, Spiritual Teachers, Group Councils, Deities and benevolent Extraterrestrials as Angels. They are not.

The Cosmic Council of Light, Ascended Masters, the Sirian-Pleiadean Alliance are unified entities that operate generally in Councils. These are representative and advisory disciplines that express tenets, principles, theories and beliefs associated with a body of knowledge. The Cosmic Council of Light is composed primarily of highly advanced beings who have experienced and completed the lessons of physical duality and have chosen to empathically assist humanity. Likewise, many of the Sirian-Pleiadean Alliance have experienced life on Earth.

God's Image

There are myriad life forms of Divine Intelligence in the Cosmos that have 'bodies' vastly different from the forms you have on Earth. These are also created in 'God's Image.' And so understand that the image of God that is life is conscious Light, is LOVE.

The Angelic Realm

Dear Ones, the state of 'Enlightenment' is just that, it is Beingness within Light ... Integral Coherent Crystalline Light. The Ascension is around the Crystalline transition of the planet Earth. In kind, this crystalline transition makes available not only greater access to higher dimensions but also the shift of humanity into Mer-Ka-Na, Crystalline Light Body. The Mer-Ka-Na is able to absorb more light, you see, and thus allows you to carry greater energy as you become capable of interfacing more synergistically into crystalline dimension and the Angelic Realm.

The Angelic Kingdom is greatly misunderstood in certain aspects of its nature and core purpose. Angels are indeed 'Messengers of God.' But what does that mean?

Angels are Multidimensional Beings of Light that serve a far greater function than guardianship and bearing of messages. We will attempt to review the greater aspect of Angels, but before we do, we will tell you that Angels as Beings of Light are conscious Beings of the Divine Essence of the key frequency for assisting humanity to evolve ... and that is Love. We add the caveat that Love is a frequency far more complex and much, much higher than just the emotional feeling you think of as love. LOVE is a complex science.

As we have told you previously, the highest form of Love is 'Unconditional Love.' And while Unconditional Love can be sought from the stance of the 3rd dimension, it can only be grasped from the level of the 5th dimension. That is because Unconditional Love is integral, and the 3rd dimension is a conditional (not unconditional) plane. Those of you who achieve the initial aspects of Unconditional Love only do so on the level of the 5th dimension, you see.

Angels As Place Holders of Physics

You think of Angels as nurturing guardians, messengers of 'God.' We are that and more. Most of you will agree that Angels are 'Beings of Light.' In the latter definition you encompass a Truth that is vastly more far reaching than the initial description. Beings of Light, Angels, are the place holders of the Laws of Physics, conscious in scopes you cannot even imagine.

Angels have a reciprocal nature and aspect in dimensional Light, meaning that Angelics exist within the field of antimatter in Fractal Light and fold inward into physical realms in Geometric Light. In so doing they are core energetic holders that consciously hold the special laws of dimensions intact.

Angels are without form, occupy no physical space; in your terms we have no mass. We are Divine Thought and intact in manifestation. We are 'tonal' and have a spectrum of frequency at our disposal. That frequency is LOVE.

We tell you that there is both a plural and a singular aspect within the Angelic Realm. And while it may seem paradoxical, even the 'singular' aspect of Archangels is plural in consciousness content. Accordingly, individual names humanity assigns to Archangels are more to do with humanity's limited concept of Angelic attributes than to an individual Beingness. You interpret Angelics and Light Beings as having 'personalities' and gender. We are indeed 'personable' in our intermeld with humanity, and while that aspect absolutely is endearing and nurturing, we are non gendered. That which you interpret as 'personality' is the nurturing of the vibration of home.

In Truth, we are reflections of attributes of the most powerful energy in the Cosmos, and that is LOVE. Yet our essence is received and interpreted to humanity in duality as having attributes you logically consider to be individual personalities.

We are Divine Mind with loving nurturing aspect, devoid of ego, devoid of that which you term negative emotion. We support, we hold energy in place and do so as a fundamental purpose. Love is our foundation.

Humanity's Angelic Images

Although humanity assigns gendered names to Archangels, the Angelic Realm is androgynous; in your terms, neither male nor female. Because you consider certain attributes of LOVE, such as nurturing and compassion, as feminine and attributes such as strength to be masculine, you give gender to Angelics. Gender only exists in polarity.

Even the energies you refer to as 'Mother Earth' and 'Divine Mother' are labeled as female because you assign nurturing as a female characteristic. Such terms, such syntax are attached to polarity concepts and in the greater paradigm are somewhat constrictive and limiting of the true integral nature in the greater paradigm opening in 2012.

We are far above polarity. We are integral. The Beings of Light that are of the Angelic Realm are plural / multidimensional forms of integral conscious energy. Our plurality consciousness is the reason we often do not refer to ourselves or relate our messages to you in the 'I' of singular pronoun. Yet, in seeming paradox, we are also singular in unification.

Humans tend to create images of Angels that are responsible to some degree for the misconceptions around their true nature. Your paintings and murals depict either muscular male figures, females with feathered wings or a host of miniature cherubs. Angels are neither male nor female in their Beingness. Gender is an aspect of polarity / duality. And, of course, Angels do not have wings, feathers or even the grandiose humanesque forms. We are by no means offended by such images, these are simply artists' mental images that replicate and reinforce some of the misconceptions.

Many of your religious texts and scriptures tell you that 'God' created mankind in 'His' own image. You even see 'God' as a patriarchal male with a humanesque body. It is the same mental thought process that logically depicts Angels as having human form. Such celestial images powerfully influence your thoughts and emotions, and thus it is natural that you create understandable images to facilitate your interfacing with the Divine.

It may be of interest for you to know that Dolphins in your oceans 'see' Angelics as having a dolphin form. In truth, Angelics are formless light. Each life form perceives them in filtered interpretation that allows for familiar interface.

Coming Full Circle

None of your present major religions offer the 'full circle,' the complete truth on the veritable nature of your reality. Each holds a piece but is riddled with inaccurate insertions. None even acknowledges the obvious premise of humanity's true 'extraterrestrial' heritage. Most speak in skewed metaphor. Many seek control through archaic fear and reinforce mental programming that obstructs avenues of self empowerment by instilling the concept of original sin and fires of hell and damnation. All of Humanity are Beings of Light, powerful spiritual consciousness, that are sparks of the Divine. The difference between Humanity and Angels is that Humans are an aspect of the Divine that evolves back into God expansion plurality, having chosen to experience free will and relearn creation through that magnanimous lens.

Angels ARE, exquisitely and splendidly ARE, and always have been 'Keepers of Light,' place holders of this space and non space of the eternal expanding 'NOW' of Alpha and Omega.

Supreme Gestalt

We will also tell you that the religious teaching of 'Fallen Angels' is also a fear based inaccuracy. There is indeed a 'Conscious Keeper' of the specific Law of Physics that enables polarity / duality, which is the force that enables the 'University of Earth.' And within that school of the duality causal plane, humanity is able to master the responsibility of creative forces.

There are no evil or fallen Angels! Period. There is no vengeful God in the heavens. There are no Angels to fear. Rather, it is a magnificent family partner with a hand reaching out to you. A familiar hand from home. It is indeed a skewed, archaic misunderstood analogy of the duality force.

The only demons, the only evils that exists in duality planes are those created by inaccurate thought in the learning process of 'free-will.' Demons are your creation within the opposing fields of polarity.

There are no 'fallen angels.' How could a Being of Light created by Divine Source divert from what it is? Angels do not have 'free-will,' in your terms. Rather, they have Divine Will.

The Supreme Gestalt of 'All That Is' is the substance of the reality that underlies all appearances and manifestations that are called Life, including matter, antimatter, non matter, energy and non energy, thought and the absence of thought. And we tell you that there is that which exists even beyond this.

You may not fully comprehend this axiom from your duality perspective or perhaps do not feel that this is within your field of conception, yet I would tell you otherwise. But it is ever your discernment that must be honored in order to expand as you grow into greater awareness of your God Self.

James Tyberonn

The Coded Nature of Light

The Earth is diversely luminous, receiving and disseminating light in a variety of unique frequencies, formats and bandwidths, each offering its own benefits and qualities. Light contains information, codes and colors in its spectrum of varied oscillations which support the Earth and indeed Humanity.

While the Sun of your solar system is the primary source of light received on the Earth, it is important to note that it is by no means the only source. Other sources include the Great Central Sun, stars, white holes and 'Light Beings.' In a valid manner of speaking, Light Beings, those far beyond your scope of Angels, provide a light that is unimaginable to you. We add the caveat that all light from all sources has a natural filtering matrix and dimensional spectral distribution.

Most humans are only able to 'physically' perceive quanta of light that occur in the 'visible range' of the light spectrum. You are aware that humans require sunlight to sustain healthy physical bodies, yet we tell you that the beings that live in the 'inner earth' also receive light as a necessary nutrient. (We offer an angelic wink as we give a wry notification that many of the planets in your particular corner of the Cosmos, including the Earth, have more advanced 'humanesque' life-forms internally than on the surface.) So, what is the source of their sustaining light? It is a polychromatic light emitted from the crystalline core of the Earth, well above the 'visible' range.

Polychromatic 'Whole-White' Light works directly with the 12 chakras of the Mer-Ka-Na. It is pristine and complete, containing all frequencies, all spectra, all creation codes in both wave and particle format. Sunlight does not. You will in time inhabit the 'Inner Earth.' The 2012 completion of the Crystalline Grid will bring changes to the way the Earth and mankind will receive light. The 144-Grid will begin over the next two to three centuries to influence the direction of light waves. It will have the capacity to attract, refract and disseminate light from one dimensional medium into another.

Carbon Base to Silicon Base

The wave velocities received will be different from the velocities refracted. It will be capable of singular and double refraction. It will be capable of refining polychromatic light into singularly coherent factions and coherent polychromatic light. New forms of crystalline and non polar morphous light will be emitted.

The grid itself will breathe, and that respiration will enact even more complex geometries beyond the double penta dodecahedron of the 144-Grid. The physical matrix of humanity will symbiotically evolve, as a direct result, into formats that embed and spawn greater abilities to retain morphic coded light. The body will become a source of light appearing semitranslucent, less fixed in density, mass and gravity. Humans will physically evolve from carbon based life to silicon based. It is crystalline Illumination, for silicon is unique in its crystalline symbiosis to light itself.

A New Sun

Masters, the Earth, Sun and all of the stellar and planetary bodies in your Cosmos are conscious and are, in that consciousness, an aspect of the Angelic Realm, albeit specialized. And even so, evolution is occurring especially in your solar system.

Your sun is changing. It has been a conditional sun in aspect to the Earth. It has played an unperceived role in the duality aspect of Planet Earth since the fall of the firmament. When the new 144-Crystalline Grid completes in 2012, it will begin to create the seeds of the New Firmament.

This will, in kind, allow for the sun to provide 'Unconditional Light.' The very manner in which humanity absorbs light will up shift, as will the ability to perceive above the current visible spectrum limitations.

The Crystalline Transition of the Earth is the base source of the planetary Ascension. It offers greater light, more complex light to humanity. Accordingly, a greater aspect of light is becoming available to humanity, and light removes shadow and offers greater understanding.

The Angelic Realm is an enormous part of your expanded awareness in the Ascension. It is time to open to the true nature of what is Angelic.

Discernment is Key

Think NOT that we desire to forcefully impose or have you change your chosen stance on God, religion or the nature of your own being. Your beliefs, values and chosen opinions are sacred steps of your free will and are fully endorsed by the 'All That Is,' of which you are a Divine Aspect.

The mode and manner, the expediency and format of your evolution is your own creation, and that is by individual design. There can be no other way to complete the University of Earth. It is not the role of the Angelic nor the Ascended Masters Councils to make choices for you; we are holders of information that you may utilize, refashion, reject or accept. It is your choice, and we tell you that each of you will graduate in time. Love is ever the key, and cause and effect are great and greater teachers that all of you will learn from.

Experiencing duality and learning Mastery en route is why you entered the course.

Closing

Masters, a beautiful completion is occurring on the Earth. It is a sacred event that all of you have cocreated. It is time that you illuminate to the great and greater aspect that has always been within you. The dreamer is awakening. The expansion of Light is the expansion of Truth, of Understanding, and it is the doorway to the return home. Like the Angels, you are Beings of Light. As yet, most of you have no idea how important you are and how the evolution that you have created in your selves has expanded the Cosmos. Before we complete, we ask you to do something very special. Take a moment and direct your energy to feel the energy of Light, of Angels.

Now ... Feel us.

Be absorbed in this angelic countenance of peace and well being. It is a moment of solace, is it not? It is the energy of Source, of home, of Light, of Love. It is Angelic, and you, Dear Ones, are feeling the frequency of our nature ... of your source nature in Angelic Beingness of Sacred Light.

It is nice, isn't it?

Every Enlightened Being who has walked the Earth in final Mastery exuded an energy that feels a lot like what you just felt. People were attracted to them, loved them. All life responded, blossomed in their presence. They created joy effortlessly, because that is the energy of LIGHT ... and, Dear Ones, you are human angels and can and will evolve in kind as you return home.

James Tyberonn

And in that sacred path, we of the Angelic Realm honor you. We await you and promise to leave the lights on for your serendipitous return.

I am Metatron, and I share with you these Truths. You are Beloved.

And so it is... AA Metatron via James Tyberonn

Our United Nations Experience ~ Metatron Channel at the United Nations: "The Nation of Humanity"

It was an auspicious day when we arrived in New York City to bring the message and wisdom of Archangel Metatron to the United Nations group. In little over a week we would be in Britain, and New York would be shaken by a rare earthquake and washed in the winds of a hurricane. But August 19th was a magnificent summer day, resplendent with blue skies and a golden beaming sun.

The UN Staff had debriefed us on security detail and entry protocol. We were ready.

This was not our standard fashion of presenting Metatron, and the unique energy of the honor and event filled us with anticipation. We had been given permission to bring a few guests.

We were met outside the UN complex, greeted graciously by UN S.E.A.T. staff and presented with a stunning arrangement of flowers. We then were escorted through the security facilities where we needed to pass through metal detectors, under the thorough gaze of uniformed United Nations security officers.

Anne and I were excited and humbled with the honor of this invitation, and amazed at how Archangel Metatron had somehow orchestrated such a marvelous opportunity as this. Anne and I paused for a moment and understood that we were representing Earth-Keepers around the globe in perhaps the only venue that would ever enable and allow governments to speak together of such things as spiritual enlightenment and the quantum physics of multidimensionality. And Metatron is about the science of Spirit, the physics of metaphysics.

The moment was very significant to us both. It had been a long journey, and not always an easy one. Although I had recently retired in 2009 from 33 years as a professional Geological-Engineer, metaphysics has always been my passion, and I had studied intensely for 35 years. I began channeling Metatron in 2007, and he had foretold of this day, and its manifestation had an enormous effect on both of us.

We passed the Security Council chambers and the large popular General Assembly meeting room. Scheduled to begin at precisely 1:15, we were to end within 90 minutes. It was a rigid agenda, with much to cover in a short span of time. The Metatronic teachings were presented, and as time approached for our ending channel, our allotment was extended. We remained three hours and finished with a channel. We were told this was the longest session the S.E.A.T. had ever allowed. As 'chance' would have it, the meeting scheduled to take place in our conference room after our 90 minutes had been rescheduled, but then again there are no accidents ... only Cosmic Winks!

Both Anne and I were feeling the powerful and beautiful presence of the Metatronic entourage of Spirit in a way that we had not previously experienced. Something very profound was happening, and it felt right. This was, in many ways, the "confirmation" that Metatron had told us about so many times.

Somehow this day at the United Nations in new York City helped me gain greater understanding in the global acceptance of what we do, and I am humbled and deeply thankful for that.

As we ended the meeting, several people from Russia and the Ukraine approached and ask me to sign their books. I was surprised to see for the first time copies of one of Metatron's books in Russian. It had been published in the Ukraine the year prior, and it was apparently responsible for igniting the interest and triggering the invitation of Earth-Keeper and Metatron to the UN, as the story was told to us. We were invited to Russia to offer live teachings in Moscow.

With Humility, Gratitude and Love,
James Tyberonn

"The Nation of Humanity"
Archangel Metatron Channel via James Tyberonn

Greetings! I am Metatron, Lord of Light, and I embrace you with love, unconditional love.

And so this wonderful day we gather at the United Nations. We pause to fill the room with the Cosmic Light of Unconditional Love. And we tell you it is only Unconditional Love that will unite nations of your beloved Earth.

We encircle each and every one of you with a nurturing energy and with the field of self empowerment, for each of you are truly Masters on your path of Ascension. It is our purpose to offer you inspiration and clarity, but indeed it is once and always requisite that YOU, as a sacred and sovereign BEING, practice discernment with this and any such 'channeled' messages.

And so it is 2011, the cusp of your heralded Ascension. And so we gently ask all of you to look at the world around you for just a moment. What do you see ?

Your media outlooks are reporting war, famine, disasters and economic collapse. And what is broadcast is what is seen in 3-D. It is oft full of gloom and doom, is it not?

But we tell you there is a new sun dawning, and it is indeed the sun of change. It brings the light of the magnificent New Earth. And, Dear Ones, we do mean magnificent.

And yes, we know that some of you are thinking, "The Angels are viewing the world with rose colored glasses. Their perspective is a Pollyanna wash."

There have always been the naysayers on the planet, those who predict gloom and doom and warnings of fear. And these serve a purpose in duality, and certainly a quick glance around the globe would seem to justify their stance. But we tell you it is old energy. And it is not the role of Spirit to ever tell you to give up hope or to let go of your free will. Our message is to tell you of your Divinity and to tell you as a matter of fact, as a point of truth that the planet and indeed humanity will Ascend ... and are absolutely on track for that to happen. Period.

The United Nations S.E.A.T.

Now, we will speak this day at the United Nations in the same vernacular that we speak to all seekers, to all aware audiences. We recognize those of you within the Society for Enlightenment and Transformation as members of the 'Transformational Team.' We know you very well, and we honor you for the roles you are playing in this organization.

The Beginning ... Not the End

So many are asking, what really will happen in 2012? The doomsday prophets are especially in high gear on this topic, are they not? Some of your speculators are on particularly fertile ground in this arena, generating fear around collisions of comets, asteroids, cataclysmic polar reversals and economic collapse.

Dear Ones, we tell you again that the Ascension will occur, and humanity has made it so. It is time to let go of old energy, of FEAR. And those of you in this room today must be leaders by example in this process.

Masters, planetary changes will occur, but they are appropriate, and the global cataclysm that some seers have predicted will NOT happen. The planet will Ascend, and humanity will be in tow. In your higher consciousness, that level above fear, not only are you aware of this ... you scripted it. And so we say, 'Well Done!"

Now, be aware that there will indeed be the cleansing of the planet, the upshifting of frequency, but it will be on a regional level, and it is for the higher good. We assure you that were it not for the regional quakes, shakes, winds and waves, devastating as they are, the larger one would inevitably have to take place. And that will not occur precisely because of the gradual shifting. It makes sense, does it not?

Letting Go Of Old Energy

Dear Ones, we tell you again that the Ascension will occur, and humanity has made it so. It is time to let go of old energy, of FEAR.

The fear is deeply programmed, but it is a repeating recording. So many of your religions are rife with embedding of fear controlled dogma, warnings and restrictions. They program you with erroneous concepts of 'original sin,' poverty vows and focus on what not to do. Their fear based controls have underpinnings of punishment for violators, creating group thought forms to cage you in. This encourages fanaticism and zealotry. It spawns self righteousness and threats of retribution: our way or else. It is old energy, it is fear. Masters, you can never return to states of lesser awareness; life is expansion.

With the New Earth comes the greater role in cocreation of the reality around you. But that is a responsibility that will enfold through love, not dread.

While you are indeed accountable for your actions, that accountability is to SELF. You are a sovereign spark of the Divine.

Greater Access to Creatorship

So what will happen in 2012? The short answer is that greater access to your divine creativity will occur. The Earth will amplify into 12 dimensions, and by having access to those crystalline fields, you employ greater ability to responsibly create.

As you enter the Ascension, the Crystalline Grid replaces the magnetic grid that has dominated Earth's ebb and flow for eons. As a result, 3rd dimensional polarity is optimally constricted within a more stabilized energy matrix.

What does that mean, Metatron, you ask? It means that the arc swing of duality will gradually lessen. And it is a gradual process; it will happen on time-release.

And we tell you that it has already begun. That is precisely why the old energy holdouts are kicking hard. They are drawn out of the shadow into the crucible for all to see. As the light grows brighter, the bugs will be attracted to it. But events can no longer be skewed to hide the truth. Look at what is happening *in North Africa. Positive change is happening, and much more is to come. That we assure you.*

United Nations

And so we say to all of you gathered here that the S.E.A.T. carries an important role, perhaps more important than even those of you here realize. For you are the voice of those who cannot speak, and you have the ears of those who will listen. And many within the delegation will listen to you. So do not be discouraged, for we recognize your importance, even if others do not.

We tell you that at any given time, half the world is in light and half the world is in night; it is a world of polarity. We say to you that far more than half of humanity are in consciousness shadow, yet to awaken to the light of wisdom. We tell you that enlightenment occurs one heart at a time.

Therefore, the light bearers among you must never lose faith, must ever shine brightly, for even a small photon wave makes a transitional illumination. So it is, so it must be with you here today.

1st World Nations

Now, there are some that will say that the prominent nations of that which you term the 1st world, the financially dominant and powerful, are more like corporations than countries. Corporations based on profits whose residents are treated more as employees than citizens, especially within the United States.

That the gap between the ' haves and have-nots is growing increasingly wider. There are some that would say that the overall masses of the United States are controlled and manipulated by media, intoxicated by quantity and enslaved by debt. That sovereignty of the individual has been lost. Yet a light still shines, and it is growing brighter. A new generation across the planet are coming into power, and they will quicken the change. We tell you that the time is nearing in which people will awaken to the knowledge that it is not their encumbering debt that ties them to their beliefs, rather their beliefs that shackle them to the burden of debt.

The global economic system will change, but it will not free fall and crash irreparably in planetary chaos. To do so in utter chaos would not serve what is to come. Rather it will be forced into change, drastic change, and positive elements will come forward to enable a better way.

The New Earth, the New Humans cannot and will not create their better future by simply discarding their past. The change will come by learning from the past and adjusting in the present, one step at a time. The new Humans in the generations that are coming into power in the next decade will choose a new pattern as a work in progress, and that economic shift will occur.

The Power of Love

Masters, we have said before and we say again that when the love of power is replaced by the power of love, humanity will make a quantum leap. But know that love without strength is incomplete. Love without strength is not integral LOVE.

The changes the next 15 generations of humanity will make will create the flowering of the Ascension.

Change is occurring all around you, and it is not hard to see. Look at what has happened and is happening even now in North Africa and the Middle East. And look at how this shift began. It took strength, it took will, it takes courage. This is what we mean when we say integral LOVE requires strength, and that strength was an accomplishment of great will and courage.

The Strength of Love

One courageous young man in Algeria decided enough was enough, and he wasn't going to take the injustice of tyrannical corruption anymore. He extinguished his life with a flame, and that fire burnt into the face of tyranny ... and it is still burning. A purifying crucible. Look at what the actions of one pure soul created; it spawned a revolution that is still turning wheels and changing the world.

The energy of the planet is changing, and the 'old guard' of political power over love simply cannot stand in the new paradigm. Nations that rule by brute force are falling, one tyrant, one corrupt government at a time.

And so we say to all governing bodies that unless change is brought from the top, it will be summoned from the bottom, and mightily so.

A New Accounting

Governments must be of the people and by the people. Governments must care for the least of their populace and not be templates of power play for greed and cunning. Heart and love is the new energy, this is the new way, this is the new accounting.

Governments cannot sit on thrones and watch carelessly as their citizens struggle to survive. Nations of the 1st world are required to lift the 3rd. But not by military means, not by corporate manipulation. Through sharing. Through understanding that a human life cannot be measured in gold or derogated into ineffectuality by lack of it.

And what of the economy? Look at what has happened in the past five years. Dear Ones, Spirit is not short of cash. There is a means for all to have abundance. There is a prerequisite for each soul to have the opportunity of life.

And truth cannot be hidden, the shadow is being removed. Manipulation is manipulation, and corruption is corruption, even if it is for the short term hidden in shadowed legalities and sham. The current economic system will morph into a different one in time.

The Middle Path

The middle road between that which is termed capitalism and that termed socialism will in time be realized and in time prove the more tenable way. Life is about gain, but gain is not always about monetary profit. Yet, learning to create is part of your puzzle on the Earth plane in duality, and you have and will in time experience every path along the road to the solution of sharing the planetary resources.

War and Conflict

As 2012 approaches, mankind is weary of war, but not enough are yet empowered to force their leaders to stop it. In days past, wars were formed in royal courts and political temples. In current times, wars are created in executive military-corporate board rooms.

The victims are but a brief mention in the evening news alongside stock reports. Rarely do countries decide in free majority will to go to war, but they blindly accept their leaders who declare them. If you were to open the curtains of your hidden history, you *would know that most of your planet's conflicts of war do not occur in happenstance, rather they are strategically chosen. There are no enemies to defend against, rather strategies designed to fill bank accounts and increase power reach.*

War is an aspect of polarity that will only end as the Earth and humanity rise above it. Hating war will never end war. Loving peace will end war by creating peace.

Dear Ones, so much is changing, can you not see that a great shift is taking place? Could this be what is called the Ascension?

And so, what is this 2012 Ascension? What will happen in 2012?

The Planetary Ascension

Dear Ones, for most of the planet, Dec 21st will come and go, and the world will say nothing has changed. If you are hearing these words in hopes that the final phrases of this discussion will weave a conclusion to your liking, you will not be disappointed.

But we tell you that while the template of expansion occurs in 2012, the mass enlightenment of mankind will not follow for several centuries. 2012 simply gives you more tools to work with.

We of the Angelic realm are not here to solve your problems, rather to encourage you on your path to solution.

And although mankind will not reach a critical mass of enlightenment on the Earthplane for several more centuries, it is important to remain present and positive, because it will occur, one day at a time, one heart at a time.

James Tyberonn

Each of you has an opportunity to be impeccable every day. The scenario in which you recognize your own failings, your own conflict with integrity is the day you encompass Mastery, and indeed, it is a journey. Likewise, the day you stand in your truth with willingness to recognize another person's truth, you encompass integrity. This truth then applies to nations as well, it applies in macro and micro.

Spirit speaks of LOVE. Spirit does not attack. Every current religion on your Earth has its truths and distortions. Discernment is the key. It is requisite of you to decide what is true and what is not, based on heart and NOT FEAR. No true sacred expression limits its truth, its beauty, to one grouping.

Dear Ones, choose to live free, choose to release worry and fear, and create your own well-being. Respect and nurture one another, and embrace LOVE. It is the science and frequency of God. It is the way that the Nation of Humanity will UNITE.

I am Metatron, and I share with you these TRUTHS. You are Beloved.

And so it is... AA Metatron via James Tyberonn

Animal Consciousness ~ The Divinity of Cats and Dogs, The Sacred Felidae
Archangel Metatron Channel via James Tyberonn

Greetings Masters! I am Metatron, Lord of Light, and I embrace you in this moment. With me are the energies and presence of the Angelic Realm, the Ascended Masters of the Cosmic Council of Light and those benevolent Beings of the Sirian-Pleiadean Alliance. We welcome you, each of you here in a 'Now' moment of unconditional love.

Dear Ones, with the understanding that you are here for learning, we tell you that the 'University of Polarity Earth' is specifically designed for the evolution of the human soul. The curriculum and venue of Polarity Earth, the educational process is in fact a version of the Omni-Earth that is created and cocreated in Divine Intelligence. It is a purposed illusion, it is created by purposed thought and cannot be destroyed. Consider that. That does not mean you do not have responsibilities in the care of Earth and its supporting Kingdoms, for indeed that is part of the learning process.

The purpose of the Earthplane is your soul evolution. The Earth supports that mission by Divine plan, by agreement, and all of the Kingdoms of Earth are part of that. Accordingly, we tell you that there are versions of other Beings that are of Divine Intelligence that are here to support you in your purpose here.

These include Master Beings from many realms. Some make visitations here to support you, and some chosen of these come in full avatar consciousness. But be aware that there are versions of benevolent Master Beings that have by agreement chosen to manifest in various step-down forms to support humanity.

Those of the Animal Kingdom on the Earth are here to support you. Part of that process involves their expression on the

James Tyberonn

Earthplane in 'Group' Consciousness. The deepest dimensions of the animal self exist not at the level of the individual but of the entire species, and that highest level is not enrolled in the duality lesson, per se.

And so we speak this gathering of the Sacred Felidae of Sirius A. The Sacred Felidae and Canidae are incredible Beings that bring tremendous support to the Humanity.

The Felidae are Divine Intelligence, fully evolved, magnificently conscious in crystalline expression. They are members of both the Sirian-Pleiadean Alliance and of what may be termed the Niburian Mastery Council. Both of whom are benevolently involved in the upshift of the consciousness evolution of planets and planetary races who are prepared to graduate into the next level in their Ascension.

The Felidae

The Felidae are a Feline species who originate on Sirius A. These are Beings that have entered the Earthplane since ancient times in specific roles and formats. The versions currently in physical form on the Earthplane are in what may be termed the Feline and Canine family. These physical formats on the Earthplane are here to support you and in their physical matrix are but a portion of the consciousness of their Sirian nature.

That is because the Felidae expression on the Earth are in group soul format and are not here to evolve as a species, but rather to support the Earth and assist humanity in evolution. The greater part of their consciousness is above the level of the Earthplane. The feline operate vastly in the ethereal or stealth antimatter realm. Their full consciousness existed and manifested in LeMurian, Atlantean and early Egyptian eras.

The Masters of the Sacred Felidae were involved in the genetic engineering in the Temple of Purification (on Poseida) in Atlantis during the Golden Age of the Law of One. This was done in a very positive and benevolent manner, prior to such technology being tragically misused by the Aryan Sons of Belial in the sad demise of the final era of Atlantis.

The Felidae of Sirius A and Cetacean Sirian B Masters are skilled at integrating spirit into physical matter. This in not only giving life force to a physical form, but also in integrating higher chakric levels of consciousness within the physical matrix in Mer-Ka-Na level multidimensionality.

This ability to work with humanity in energetic terms involves activating higher chakras and higher crysto-light bodies. This higher level of consciousness is the Crystos Consciousness, and the Cetaceans are Crystalline Masters. Their renewed role on the Earth includes assisting the shift-transition from the declining magnetic polarity grid to the evolving Crystalline Grid.

Question to Metatron: *So are the Beings from Sirius B primarily aquatic, and the Beings from Sirius A Feline?*

AA Metatron: *The habited realm circulating Sirius B is primarily aquatic, and the Cetaceans, the Dolphin and Whale are aquatic. Yet also of a high enough consciousness to manifest form that can equally habituate within both aqueous realms and that which would be termed land.*

The life-forms of the sister star, Sirius A, are different expressions than the Cetaceans. Sirius A enlivens Humanoid Life (Starseed), as well as the Sacred Starseed Felidae. These are all Beings of Divine Intelligence, that all have varied expressions supporting the Earthplane. These all interact with your planet on many levels in myriad forms.

James Tyberonn

Question to Metatron: *You have mentioned that only humans are in soul evolution on planet Earth. Aren't the dolphins and whales also in a high state of consciousness and evolution?*

AA Metatron: *The Sacred Cetaceans are indeed in a high state of evolution. But they are not on the Earth to evolve. They are already evolved. So understand they are here on the Earth to support the Earth and assist mankind in so doing. The Cetacean are physically here to anchor the energy in the aquatic portions of the Earth to enable the planetary balance and to facilitate the shift from magnetic to crystalline. The etheric, nonphysical, return of the 'Golden Dolphin' are the Sacred Cetaceans in full avatar Mastery, directly assisting humanity to evolve into Crystalline Mer-Ka-Na field.*

The Felidae are assisting humanity in physical manifestation but have also assisted in etheric Mastery, particularly in Atlantis, Central America and Egypt. But in the stepped-down form, they assist you in emotional and mental fields, and this is the primary topic of today's discourse, that of the Felidae in expression of Feline and Canine.

Question to Metatron: *I am intrigued by the information on the Felidae and Canidae of Sirius A. Are you speaking of cats and dogs? Can you expand on this?*

AA Metatron: *Certain breeds of what may be termed house cats and dogs are indeed uniquely designed derivations of the Starseed Felidae. They perform specific roles in assisting humans. The 'house' versions of cats and domestic dogs are genetically engineered from the Golden Age of Atlantis.*

The genetic engineering was benevolently done by the Sirian-Pleiadean Alliance and is an extremely helpful action, as stated to assist humanity as they became more densely ingrained in the

Earthplane. Now, that which you term as canine and feline are of the same source, both are derivations of the Starseed Felidae. Cats and dogs are different physical forms of the same source.

The Felidae of Sirius A are a fully conscious crystalline being. They have melded into a group unity consciousness, yet still retain aspectual individual identities with the greater harmonic field. The Group Field chooses to assist humanity in your Universe and others.

Cats and Dogs

Both cats and dogs in this derivation are serving as benevolent energy giving assistants to humans, to their caretakers. Both have the capacity to meld their energy fields with the human and are uniquely capable of becoming personality fragments of their human caretakers. That is why certain of these can often begin to display the physical characteristics of their 'owners,' although this particular aspect occurs more commonly with the canine.

The canine exudes an extreme loyalty and unconditional love, a dedication that energetically is received by the human, and can assist in many ways. The dogs (and cats) become companions and healers as well as protectors. The feline, the cat is much more in the ethereal (antimatter) realm in its conscious field. That is why many past societies worshiped the Feline forms of Jaguar, Lion, Tiger and Puma.

These beings are extremely aware of thought forms of ethereal realms and offer a stealth strength and protection. The house cat is capable of tremendous protection for their caretakers from untoward thought forms and negative energies. Certain breeds of dogs have this ability as well, but it is expressed and enacted differently.

Vibrational Healing

The purring of a cat is very beneficial in healing, repairing and protecting the human aura. The mystical aspect of cats has long been recognized, and 'Temple Cats' were used in many ancient societies as well as for companions and allies of the shaman.

The Lupus and other canine species such as the wolf have this ability as well. Both cats and dogs have capacity to sense and see in far greater dimensionality than the human eye. The therapy and service of cats and dogs in working with abused children, terminally ill patients, the depressed and the elderly in nursing homes are examples of significant pet therapy healing being more and more recognized. This will be expanded even further in the future.

Cats see above visible light and can actually see the human auric field, the Human EMF and all manner of energy emanations invisible to the human eye. The wide spectrum that cats perceive in light fields is quite amazing. Cats see in fields of both nonphysical matter and non matter. Cats also are uniquely able to assist humans in not only better understanding of their dreams and dream world interludes ... but also capable of assisting you in more lucid awareness while in an ongoing dream, in other words, greater conscious clarity during dream-states.

Dogs are more in the field of matter; they sense or feel these auric fields and indeed are extremely capable of understanding the direct resonance of the human emotional field. Additionally, Felidae 'canine' dogs assist in helping humans better understand their feelings and emotional blockages and help humans work through them into a better state of balance. We will speak more on these attributes further into this discussion.

The service of 'Seeing Eye' dogs with the blind is another area of service in which great bonds are created. Dogs are able to 'feel' and indeed smell dis-ease within the human body. They will often lay their own bodies in the area of the human malady and transfer energy to assist in rebalancing the area of imbalance. They will also mentally project awareness to the human of the malady in direct telepathic communication.

Cats will provide a similar service, but their sense of the human imbalance is visually observed. A cat sees the human auric field in great clarity, in vivid color and detail. Areas of malady will appear discolored to the feline. The cat will often lay on the area and purr or exude a balancing frequency or color to assist the rebalance.

Unique Melding With Human Consciousness

The version of Felidae and Canidae that are cats and dogs are but a fragment of the full consciousness and energy spectrum of their Sirian aspects. Yet, this expression is specifically and purposefully designed to be so, for these beings can become so bonded with the humans they serve, that a unique third consciousness can succinctly evolve between the human and the 'pet' that is extremely beneficial to the evolvement of the human caretaker.

The Earthen consciousness of the dogs and cats operates more on thought patterns with powerful instinctual triggers. Their designed (benevolent) divinely agreed DNA engineering is such that they have a unique and divinely purposed ability to become allied, programmed in a partnership with the human they are working with.

When this partnership occurs, these beings are able to telepathically receive thought images sent by their caretaker. Just as human thought can program a living crystal, the same occurs, albeit in a different format, with dogs and cats. It may be termed as the formation of a personality aspect of the human within the cat or dog. The 'pet,' then, is capable of assisting the human in both physical and emotional ways. Thus providing comfort, energy, healing, companionship, detecting illness, sealing auric ruptures and providing protection in physical and etheric realms.

Many humans have household pets in cats and dogs that help them work through blockages. One of the most common occurrences is that these Beings help you awaken your ability to express love. It is very easy to express and give affection to the household animal, and for many this is far easier than expressing love and kindness to other humans. Depending on the individual, this blockage can occur for many reasons.

Very often as humans grow older, children move away, a spouse passes over and a seeming natural period of lonely isolation sets in. The interaction with the pet can awaken the flow of love through fond endearment. This interaction awakens the very life force in the isolated caretaker, and an interplay that is very therapeutic occurs.

We tell you that there is far more design and intelligence in the willing participation of the Felidae and Canidae than is recognized.

The Third Field Between Humans and Pets

When this third consciousness through interaction is formed, it expands the field of both parties. It awakens within it characteristics that neither of the parties involved had prior experience. In other words, it expands, it stretches the emotional field awareness, and indeed the third meld consciousness, and this reaches back into and changes the individual awareness of both. The pet opens up your ability to remain 'positive' in allowing you to express love, and you 'teach' it, in a manner of speaking, to channel the greater part of its divine Sirian consciousness in doing so.

Your willingness for the interaction allows it to achieve its specific purpose, and there is an important growth on both sides unique to the field created between the two of you. The 'pet' operated in group consciousness prior to the 'melding' blend with the human, and the individuality of it was formed in the bond with the human. Do you understand?

Question to Metatron: *Are you saying that animals are not individual unless they blend with the human to form the 'consciousness meld' with humans?*

AA Metatron: *In a manner of speaking, yes, that is what we are saying. But, to be clear, we are not saying that animals do not have individual aspects before the meld. Each are incarnate in physical bodies and are indeed subject to the gravitational characteristics, to some degree, that occur in the astrological influences in all life on the Earth. But they operate fully, and only in 'group soul' awareness, until the meld with human(s) uniquely occurs. That interaction is succinct and builds a personal fragment capable of growing. But we are not saying that animals do not have a 'group' purpose without the meld.*

The group purpose is transformed into a singular 'service' in the expanded field by means of the human interaction with the 'group' soul of the household pet as expressed in the individual cat or dog. It is therefore the human interaction that creates the individual field within the pet. So in a manner of speaking the animal has agreed to be benevolently 'programmed in blend' with the mental field, emotional field and personality of the human caretaker for higher purpose.

This is how the third field is created, and that third field is a fragment of the human consciousness that benefits both, you see. Yet, the primary purpose is to benefit the human, a service provided by the Felidae. But there is a choice to accept the human on the part of the Felidae, and when that is mutually accepted, the greater role of the Group Soul can be fed into the meld, and wisdom, protection and healing can be given from the 'pet' to the human. So understand, this third meld is a conduit that is very far reaching but occurs by agreement.

The Atlanteans, LeMurians and Egyptians in particular interacted with the Felidae in roles of guardianship and wisdom transfer. The Egyptian Temples contain many hieroglyphs depicting the Felidae, as having Feline heads and human torsos and limbs, complete with the 'Solar Disc' of enlightenment. The Sphinx is the reverse, the human head with the Feline body.

Question to Metatron: *How exactly do 'cats and dogs' offer protection to humans? Is this by their greater awareness of other dimensions?*

AA Metatron: *Yes, specifically by being much more in tune to other realms that are, as we have explained, somewhat invisible to human physical senses.*

The guardianship in the specific forms as described in 'household or human interface versions' of the Sirian Beings is performed in a beautiful manner. And that is through not only the detection of what may be termed 'negative energies' but by neutralizing those very untoward energies by powerful projections of benevolent loving energy vibrations that are orchestrated through the Sirian Felidae to the human. The Sirian being diagnoses exactly what is needed and channels the necessary vibration to assist the caretaker.

You do not always recognize that you induce auric fracturing when you become depressed or highly upset. These states form negative fields that open you to untoward auric attachments that are energetically draining.

When a cat 'purrs,' the vibration is of a deep contentment, and the frequency within that vibration is very healing, capable of evaporating negative fields by neutralizing them. Likewise, when dogs playfully jump and run, often in joyous spins, they are, like the dolphin, forming energy vortexes capable of cleansing the energies, and offering a 'channeled' frequency that is extremely beneficial to the environ, not only removing negative vibrations but creating a shield to eliminate their reentry. When cats seem to 'patrol' the perimeter of a room, house or yard, they are also exuding an immense protective field.

We will tell you that the Felidae and the Canidae, the Feline and Canine, are from the same root source of Sirius A, although their expressions on Sirius A are fully evolved. As we have told you, the household versions of these Beings are in fact physical formats, genetically engineered by the Sirians to assist humanity in the ways we are herewith discussing.

Question to Metatron: *To be clear, are you saying that cats and dogs are from the same Sirian source?*

AA Metatron: *In the higher original source, yes. Both of the one crystalline fully Evolved Mastery of Sirius A, the Felidae. Cats and dogs are from the same source. On Sirius, they are now Crystalline Light Beings, nonphysical, from your perspective, appearing in Crystalline Light forms.*

As we mentioned, the Felidae have manifested in full Avatar Mastery at various times on your planet to assist you. The Felidae are masters of incorporating Spirit into physicality and assisted in the original engineering of full strand DNA for mankind. Indeed, the races of humanity contain Sirian Felidae aspects in their DNA, some more than others. The very athleticism and agility prevalent in some humans draws on this, to give one of many aspectual examples.

Question to Metatron: *As an item of curiosity, if they are of the same Sirian source, why do dogs chase cats?*

AA Metatron: *Dogs only chase cats until they catch them. At that point, the tables usually turn, and quite quickly! (Laughter.)*

The short answer is that dogs work in the physical realm and cats more in the nonphysical ... as in matter / non matter. Both completing the opposing sides of the 'torus,' one inward, one outward.

We will say that in a real sense, dogs and cats are inverses of the same frequency when expressed on the Earthplane. That is why cats generally sleep 16 hours and are active 8 hours, and the reverse schedule is true for dogs. Generally speaking, the Feline, the domesticated cats tend to be more introverted and the Canine, dogs more external or extroverted. Their frequencies are then inward in the former, outward in the latter and naturally attract one another ... not repulse. You will find that dogs and cats raised or living in the same household develop special loving bonds. This particularly occurs in an enhanced manner when the animals have had past sojourns in which the fragment of personalities with the humans form. As an example, the channel now houses two cats and two dogs. They work together and share a deep bond, and all four are aspects of the two human caretakers. We will also add that one of the dogs, the female, has been Feline in the past more often than Canine.

The Sacred Felidae in their Earthplane manifestation have retained the unique ability to operate simultaneously in inner and outer world projections much more so than humans. At any one time in which you observe the physical material manifestation of a Felidae, they are equally conscious of being fully manifested simultaneously in other dimensional planes. Quite often they interact within the other realms while present physically in this one.

Linear Filters of Consciousness

Although humans also simultaneously exist in other levels, humans in 3-D cannot interpret the frequencies of the other realms in consistency or lucid clarity through the physical brain alone. The mind, which is the inner counterpart of the brain, can at times perceive the far greater dimensions of any given event through a crysto-electric burst of sudden intuition or comprehension that cannot be adequately described on a verbal level. The crystalline electrical impulses that are perceivable within your 3-D system is merely a tiny fraction of the vast crysto-electrical system in the Cosmos.

A human's physical brain is, on its own, quite incapable of accurate perception or deciphering of the frequencies above polarity. It is impossible in the physical brain alone to even grasp the myriad complexity and dimension of the crysto-electrical potential and actuality as it exists. And although these are quite accessible in Mer-Ka-Na via higher mind, non physical levels are not accessed by the brain alone in the human, rather they must be developed in Mer-Ka-Na through mind.

So we tell you to keep in mind, pun intended, that the true origin, the eternal source and power of your Divine Intelligence and consciousness has never been rooted in the physical. Each and every human exists in other worlds, different realities and other dimensions, and the self that you call yourself is but a small portion of your entire identity. Because of the filters inherent to the physical brain, you are capable of focusing on the physical world around you, and it is that focus that enables you to eventually master the physical plane. We assure you that there is purpose in the filtering, for if the physical brain with the ego-personality were unscreened, and thus fully aware of the vast and constant barrage of telepathic communications that do impinge upon it, it would have a most difficult time retaining a sense of identity in linear perception.

It is because of the ego consciousness that you have a powerful identity awareness of the physical realm, for you are in physical with specific purpose. But we say again, it is not your true identity in the Cosmic over view.

While in physicality the human brain is simply not equipped in linear mode to be able to make sense of the signals coming in from higher dimensions. Your standard brain cannot read them. To the brain these impulses appear to be a chaotic mélange of disconnected flash images. The ego-personality brain based in linear time cannot perceive data that is not based upon sequential continuity of moments.

Interestingly, certain of the Animal Kingdom, particularly the Felidae, can. So with this axiom that Felidae and certain Canidae do operate more effectively in other coinciding planes, we tell you that is precisely why these Beings were recognized by more aware societies as guardians. It is why a dog will bark or a household cat will move in quick reaction to energies unseen by the human eye.

Your academics understand that there are spectrums of light. You also understand that the 'average' human is only capable of physical vision in the narrow spectrum termed 'visible light.'

The Felidae and certain Canidae are capable of seeing (and sensing) in a much wider sensory range. We tell you that physical matter also occurs in spectrum waves. So are there varying spectrums of matter.

Your system of physical reality on the Earthplane is not nearly as wide-reaching or complex in relative comparison with many others. The dimensions given to the narrow spectrum of physical matter barely hint at the prolific varieties of higher nonphysical dimensions. You do not recognize as yet the nature of the nonphysical in your own Galaxy, much less the Cosmos. We tell you that Universes can exist within a molecule, and other versions of Earth validly coexist where you now sit to read these words.

The Animal Kingdom ~ Forgotten Teachers

These beings that in current terms would be considered of the 'Animal Kingdom' have taught humans far more than you presently recognize. The Beings that you term Animals operate in great and greater intelligence, albeit in a thought pattern matrix uniquely formatted to the natural aspect of the Earthplane.

On an aspectual level far more comprehensive than you currently grasp, the Animal Kingdom are here by agreement to support humanity on many levels. Their understanding of the Earthplane as a University of Development for humanity is extended from and back to their Mastery Source.

Their mental format pattern in the earthly expression is such that humans are held somewhat blameless. Although humanity does have a huge responsibility to treat the Animal Kingdom with respect, the Animal Kingdom do not place guilt on humans. Their chosen mental format upon the Earth is designed in such a manner that guilt is not an expression contained within it.

Rather it is a pattern of instinct and is benevolently capable of unconditional support.

One of the differences between the cat and dog expressions of the Felidae are that dogs are more in the physical realm than cats. From an overview, cats are far more etheric within the antimatter field while dogs much more in matter. Dogs react more to the direct frequency of your emotions, whereas cats react more to vibration and light emanations. Dogs will feel and react to anger and guilt in a more tangible way than cats. Cats cannot experience guilt, and that detachment from direct human emotional waves is why cats may seem aloof.

Animal Totems

The Animal Kingdom have a more full, vast understanding and awareness of the other conscious kingdoms of the Earth and have always had the ability to teach that to mankind. You have in current times largely forgotten, quite unfortunately, how much you learned from all of the Beings of the Animal-Kingdom. Humanity in campestral societies and cultures learned a great deal of medicine, of nutrition from watching animal behavior in interaction with the plant kingdom. Humanity observed carefully which plants to avoid and which to cultivate. You learned survival techniques and, indeed, social behavior by not only watching the animals but by directly communicating telepathically with them.

In earlier sojourns and formative epochs, mankind far more closely identified with and understood the intelligence and wisdom offered by the natural instinctual patterns of the Animal Kingdom and recognized them as wise teachers. And as a result they identified with humanity and indeed interacted with humanity to a truly remarkable degree.

The Animal Spirits or Totems recognized and honored as wisdom carriers by the Native Americans are examples of the higher group collective of their higher, off-planet consciousness etherically manifesting to assist mankind. The knowledge and intuitive communication of the Animal Kingdom with the Elemental and Devic consciousness of the Living Earth, the Mineral, Fire and Air is a precise understanding that could be of great assistance, affording forward signals to humanity in this time of Earth changes.

Question to Metatron: *You advised earlier that the Felidae Starseed are the consciousness source for both the earthen feline and canine species of animals. Do all animals on the Earthplane originate from Sirius A, from the Starseed Felidae?*

AA Metatron: *No. Sirius A is the source of humanoids and Felidae. Sirius B is the source of the Sacred Cetacean, dolphin and whale. Dolphin and whale are of the same source, the Cetacean, just as the feline and canine are of the same source, Starseed Felidae.*

Sirius is not merely two binary stars in the Cosmos with circulating planets. It is a vibrational frequency of a realm that has achieved Crystalline Ascension. It is accordingly a sacred celestial resonance and way of being within a vastly expanded consciousness. Sirius is within all dimensions both physical and nonphysical. The Stars of Sirius are portals or gateways to these other dimensions, and the Felidae, Hathor and Cetacean are here in varied matrixial expressions, assisting humanity to grow in awareness, to balance the Earth and to find their way home. The Sirians are receivers and transmitters of this divine loving energy. Other members of the Animal Kingdom in Earthen expression come from a multiplicity of sources. For example, the horse is Arcturian in source.

James Tyberonn

The Animal Kingdom have truly been your teachers, although they did not choose your 'human' evolution path. As we have said, the Animal Kingdoms are not on the Earth to evolve in soul expansion but rather to support the soul expansion of humanity.

We assure you that mankind could not have moved forward as a species had it not been for the Beings of the Animal Kingdom. Indeed, certain of the Animal Kingdom, such as the bovine and certain other species of the mammal and bird, are here by agreement to provide a food source for mankind. Does that surprise you that this occurs by agreement? And although it is not the topic at hand, the Plant Kingdom has also been a huge support to mankind.

Domesticated animals have benevolent purpose in choosing their earthen expressions. Those of the Feline and Canine have a unique role of interaction in the aspects of human companionship. This is by a higher sourced 'service' agreement. And, we will add, the enhanced ability to form the 'personality meld' in household pet derivations of the Felidae is genetically enhanced.

Interaction

Many humans find that they can interact more easily with 'pets' than they can with other humans. Pets don't talk back. The feline and canine are particularly committed to assist humans in dealing with blockage, in dealing with isolation, particularly as humans become older and alone.

Both cats and dogs oft teach humans to learn to love again and to open their hearts. Dogs are tied to the human emotional field, cats to the human psychic plane / mental field. The two are very different expressions of the Felidae, but both are focused on your assistance, both are uniquely capable of forming a fragmentation aspect of the caretaker's personality.

When a human forms a personality fragmentation meld with a Felidae or Canidae, that succinct energy can uniquely evolve and often reincarnate, or reattach within other lifetimes and within the same lifetime to continue to assist the owner. Thus a human may have the same energy essence of their cat or dog, over a span of 70 years, in several sequential cat or dog bodies. For example, the two cats and one of the dogs that the channel is caretaker for in the present were with him in different bodies as domesticated leopards in a past lifetime in Egypt.

Question to Metatron: *Pets often become family members, like children to their caretakers. And when they pass over, the caretakers are quite devastated. Can the same soul essence of the pet reincarnate immediately, if the owner obtains a new pet?*

AA Metatron: *The 'personality meld' of the pet is, in essence, a unique part of the human caretaker, a personality fragment. When a pet physically dies, the meld-fragment consciousness will absolutely remain close by in etheric planes to continue in connection to the human.*

The human is often able to sense, even see or feel the essence of the pet after it passes over, or even if it runs away or is lost. The owner can communicate with the meld personality essence, and it will indeed 'reincarnate,' reenter the body of a new pet. This is best if the new pet is obtained within two to three weeks of the passing and is the same breed as the previous pet. In a short time, the distinct personality traits and characteristics of the previous pet will clearly reemerge in the new body, and the relationship and support will continue.

In the event the new pet is a different breed and or a different astrological pattern, the similarities may not be as immediately apparent, but the meld-essence and support will be the same source. This is important to understand.

Closing

In current times, it is considered fashionable in certain circles to see mankind as the greedy destroyer of the Earth and its kingdoms, especially Animal, Plant and Mineral. It is likewise popular in some 'New Age' circles to see man as the arrogant taker who contaminates the Earth, destroys the Natural Earth Kingdoms at the expense of future generations.

We insert here that a portion of this is true, and that change is required. We do not condone humanity's untoward and irresponsible action in this issue. The point is that some who wish for the better feel that all is hopelessly lost, that change for the better will not come.

While unified determination to make change for the better is essential, the focusing on hopelessness must stop. That is the wrong application in creating the 'New Earth.' Focusing on hopelessness and despair, creates hopeless despair.

So we offer you an insight of hope.

What we wish to point out is that the Earth is the dynamic manifestation, at any given time, of your thoughts. Humanity are ever the cocreators of the Earth and Omni-Earth in all of its probable realities. We tell you, Dear Masters, the Earth is a magnificent and purposed illusion that is absolutely created by thought. Mankind en masse are, at the present time, unconscious of the fact that YOU are cocreators of the Earth experience.

There are other versions of probable reality in holographic 'time programs' in which enlightened 'Ascended' humanity honor each other, the Earth and all of her kingdoms in beautiful harmony. Duality programming of the Earthplane is intelligently and divinely planned. The 'Trial and Error' evolution of this experience takes into account the learning curve.

And, that being said, we tell you that you cannot truly destroy the Earth. You can and will create the Enlightened Earth by positive focus on its manifestation, not by focal despair that it has not yet occurred.

Nothing is taken from the Earth, or from any of the Earthen Kingdoms, Mineral, Plant and Animal that is not fully agreed to, fully permitted in the linear reality drama hologram. It rarely occurs to you that animal kingdom consciousness came into physicality and Earthen form by choice, and that the consciousnesses of such animals had a willing choice in the agreement to support humanity, fully aware of the potentials of man's stages of ignorance as humanity evolves.

In the not too distant future, humanity will come to realize and not only honor the Animal Kingdom, but equally honor, acknowledge and indeed LOVE one another and the beautiful Earth that nurtures you. It will occur. Create it as so!!!

I am Metatron, and I share with you these Truths. You are Beloved.

And so it is... AA Metatron via James Tyberonn

James Tyberonn

The Mayan Calendar and Time
Archangel Metatron Channel via James Tyberonn

Greetings! I am Metatron, Lord of Light! I embrace each of you in light, in love. Dear Ones, I know each of you, far more than you may realize. And we savor these moments we share.

And now another precious moment brings us together, uniting thoughts within the matrix of the unified field. Combining geometric thought patterns with desire, with awareness, and so do all things come together in the same way. For all thoughts, all things, all beings are representations of light, of consciousness, of manifestation, of all that ever was or ever will be.

Dear Humans, the Universe, the Cosmos is perfection itself, regardless of any dimensional interpretation or perception of it. In a quantum sense, all things in the crystalline unified field act precisely, perfectly, according to their nature, their architectural integrity. Yet some are created at higher frequencies, at higher vibratory resonance than others. And so with these words, we begin this most interesting discussion.

Question to Metatron: *According to one modern Mayan Calendar interpreter, we are in the midst of an acceleration of consciousness like no other. In fact, the researcher says that the rate of consciousness will speed up by a factor of 20 in 2011, so a shift in consciousness that took a whole year from 1999 until now will take only 20 days. This factor of 20 will be in full potential from March 9th to October 28, 2011. If this is so, what does it mean exactly?*

AA Metatron: *So to begin this discussion, we will say that the potential for increased consciousness is indeed taking place as a preset quickening of the Ascension. However, the 'rate' of shift varies with each individual, and as such a fixed factor of the acceleration cannot truly be given per se.*

Before we comment further on the acceleration of consciousness, we wish to add an interesting point to the conversation. The incredible calendar that you humans currently refer to as Mayan was not developed nor originally written by the society of Mayans in the manner that you currently attribute. Indeed, it predated the Mayans by more than 18,000 years. It was originally developed by the enlightened Atlanteans of Poseida with assistance from the Sirian-Pleiadean Alliance and stored in crystalline technology, termed the Crystal Skulls.

Even your more creative anthropologists considers the earliest Mayan society only began around 2,000 BC. We assure you that the calendar was in place and effect, in a much more expansive format, long before the Mayan society came into existence. What you now refer to as the Mayan calendar is but a small remnant of what pre existed the Mayans.

You see, the area inhabited by the predecessors of the Mayans in the Yucatan area of Mexico and Guatemala was connected by a land bridge to the Atlantean island of Poseida before the quakes and waters of the final deluge of Atlantis submerged it. Highly technically advanced cultures from Atlantis habited Central America and Egypt long before the final demise of Atlantis. The Central American, South American (OG) and Egyptian colonies and cultures emerged from and were one with the highly spiritual Atlanteans of the 'Law of One' for many millennia before the destruction of Atlantis.

These societies contained within them an elite and highly advanced group of those whom may be termed scientist-priests, the Atla-Ra These savants were highly adept at the science of mind over matter. These Masters operated through mental physics and operated in full consciousness in finesse of multidimensionality.

So while the untrained masses of humanity in the era of Atlantis lacked such skills and indeed utilized land bridges and other less advanced forms of transport to and from the colonies of Atlantis, Og, Yucatan and Egypt, the inner circle of scientist-priests had the means to etherically bi-locate and physically manifest. Not just on the physical realms of the Earth but also universally and Galactically. These savants of the Atla-Ra interacted with the extraterrestrials of the Pleiadean-Sirian Alliance and were indeed the original source of the cyclic calendar you presently term Mayan.

Small enclaves of these Master Scientist-Priests endured for millennia after the deluge and retained the knowledge of the calendar as well as the supervision of the construction of the various pyramids, with assistance from the extraterrestrials referenced. Yet, the savant priests of the Maya did not represent the society of the Mayans as a whole. That is precisely why the Mayans are an enigma to you today. Portions of the accomplishments attributed to them reveal great technical advancement, and yet the society as a whole was campestral and denigrated into unseemly ceremony involving human sacrifice and other aberrations under skewed dictatorships. Is it then quite logical to understand that the calendar pre existed the Mayan society.

So it follows, then, that the scientist-priests of OG, Yucatan, Egypt and other 'forgotten' cultures before and after them understood both the science of mental physics and had great knowledge of astronomy and dimensional cycles. Only those of adept and austere initiate traditions and societies knew this, although very little evidence of any significance remains today, and what does remain is not recognized or as yet understood.

Understanding the science of mental physics and having the ability to utilize such knowledge is what defines the gap between what your present technologies and academics know and what your advanced societies of the past knew. The influence of precise thought upon matter is not yet understood by humanity; it is a forgotten science.

The scientist-priests knew well the art of 'physical' dematerialization and remanifestation. This then, not only in terms of travel through bi-location but of physical matter ... that is indeed how the greatest of the pyramids were constructed and still remain a mystery to you today. The Atla-Ra and their descendants had the ability to mentally engineer the science of 3-D physics by shifting matter from the 3rd dimension into fields of that which may be termed antigravity to dematerialize, reform, and remanifest as substance without density. They were able under certain circumstances to alter their reality and their dimension.

These scientist-priest adepts used highly concentrated thought to reform matter into different spectrums. They understood that matter exists in spectrum waves just as light does, and they had the ability to transform into and out of different wave oscillations. Accordingly, could atomic matter be morphed to weightless vibratory states and, not only to have semi congealed mass without density, but to tangentially influence the density of both matter and its antimatter spectrum? Truly as a spectrum of the one, rather than an opposite or parallel, for matter and antimatter are part of one cycle within an integral spectrum in mutidimensionality.

The importance of this that I relate is that neither the mass populations of the Olmec, Aztec, Mayan nor the of the Mesoamerican populace retained the mastery that certain aspects of their culture exhibited. Our point is that the Atla-Ra developed the calendar, and segments of the Mayans retained that knowledge and recreated records and texts to preserve it. But just as in Atlantis, the scientist-priests, while respected, were not the governing body nor the decision makers of how the society as a whole developed.

Question to Metatron: *Is this the reason why the changes seems to come not only faster and faster but with more intensity?*

AA Metatron: *Yes, so now to return to your question and topic of 'factors of consciousness increase'...*

We will state that it is the increase in frequencial resonance that is escalating the 'potential' of each individual to shift upward into great and greater conscious awareness. The Ascension is underpinned and indeed defined by the dimensional expansion of the Earth to include the 'crystalline' realms.

The Ascension is characterized by the 'new' affording of life force consciousness units, termed by your ancients as 'Akash' or 'Adamantine Essence,' that are in themselves the potent light particulate of reality manifestation (in our terms, Consciousness Units or CUs). The crystalline realm begins at the level of the 5th dimension and extends to 15-D in humanity's paradigm of the Omni-Earth. What has existed for mankind's access prior to the dimensional expansion of the Ascension has been a transduced or 'stepped-down' version of CU's in what would be termed electromagnetic energy units that are endowed to function in the physical polarity field and linear space-time aspects of the 3rd dimension.

Crystalline consciousness units operate in a much more rapid frequency and are spurred into creative manifestation of reality through the higher aspect of mind, in the realm you refer to as the subconscious. The terms of consciousness and reality in the 3-D paradigm aspect of humanity simply cannot hold, simply cannot contain the vaster resonant context of consciousness units in crystalline dimension. Accordingly, the intensity of energies, of consciousness shift and quickening of time pulse are all attributes of the puissant resonance.

So we need to clarify and to reassert at this point that the event you refer to as the Ascension is in truth, in greater aspect the expanded availability of 3-D humanity to rise into greater dimension, the crystalline dimension that has for many millennia been unavailable in the denser physicality of humanity. Yet having the expansion of energies that make Ascension available does not mean that each individual will immediately utilize the (re)newed available opportunity. Indeed, the choice to do so remains with humanity on the micro and is the discreet, singular decision of each person. Ascension is, then, a personal option depending on the readiness, the pure intent and indeed the light quotient of the individual. Ascension, Dear Ones, occurs one heart, one mind at a time. It has always been so. For Earth is a free will, free choice environ by design.

Ascension is not a magical stardust that immediately transitions all that it touches ... rather it is a newly opened frequencial doorway that the individual may choose to pass through when ready.

Now, we will add that the energetic blend occurring on the planet at this time enhances the opportunity of consciousness to advance through the 'doorway' via a myriad blend of frequencial leaps occurring on the Earth. The energy of the planet is indeed changing, a requisite magnificent upshifting and purification is ongoing.

It is important to keep in mind that the Mayan Calendar, while very accurate in its determination of cycles, in your current paradigm can be analyzed differently by the perspective stance and light quotient of each interpreter. Accordingly, it is more accurate to say that the factor of conscious shift is determined, then, by the consciousness of the individual, and not by any preset numerical factor.

It is also tantamount to this discussion to add that certain 'Mayan' texts that were destroyed by the Spanish priests provided information that would have given far more expansive views of the calendar. We will also add that many centuries before the Maya, other texts that were tantamount to the calendar were lost in the ages and passing of linear time. Multidimensionality is not widely considered by current interpretations of the calendar, and that severely narrows and, indeed, omits the broader understanding that the enlightened scripter's of the information originally held.

The aspect of acceleration available within the Ascension, then, is not precisely predisposed to a fixed ratio, rather the rate of acceleration is determined by and actuated by the individual's intent and ability to rise into and obtain the procurable expansive energy. The concept of a 'ninth wave' is a contemporary interpretation and is not truly predicted as a preset of the 'Mayan' Calendar as established by its Atlantean originators. That does not, however, devalue its importance or the validity of its intent.

Question to Metatron: *Could you talk about this aspect of acceleration and what it offers humanity?*

AA Metatron: *Dimensional reality on the Earth is programmed to appear in a time sequence you perceive as linear. It is, in your computer terminology, a program facilitated by a server, which in this case is the 144-Crystalline Grid. Through the 144-Grid, the sub-programs of 'time' are inserted as hologramic realities. There are epochs and eras, entire civilizations that are inserted into the Grid Server as programs. That is why fully evolved civilizations such as the Mayan can seem to have* *suddenly sprung up out of nowhere into the vast 'sea of creation' within the flow of the collective unconsciousness, the consciousness grid that enables created realities.*

Linear time is a functional, purposeful illusion. In truth, all programs are running simultaneously. Therefore, on the level of the oversoul you are experiencing many civilizations and all lifetimes at the same time in the Unified Field of the Crystalline Multiverse.

An aspect of the Ascension is the apexial centering of all time, and in the greater overview the time acceleration being experienced on the planet at this time is because an aperture in the hologram programs of simultaneous time is allowing all holograms to complete themselves in this cycle. As such, that which you term 'light' is accelerating, and it affects every aspect of your current experience.

Question to Metatron: *How does it affect time, and will time disappear?*

AA Metatron: *We will say that time as you know it is indeed accelerating. Time and space are different aspects of the same energy. Both are aspects of light, and the speed of light around your planet is accelerating. Indeed, your Earth is reformulating. But, Masters, it is not merely the pulse-flash of time sequencing that is increasing, indeed, it is humanity that is increasing in vibration.*

Dear Ones, as we have told you, the world remakes itself now as the inertia of time chronology speeds past more quickly today than it did yesterday in linear sequence. Accordingly will 2011 and 2012 continue to impel the expedition of light acceleration and your lucid interpretation of consciousness.

With this surge, your cognitive expression of life will in kind shift into higher tempo. You see, the speed of light has increased, although it cannot be accurately measured by humanity at your current level of academic knowledge.

Yet as a result, it is evident to many of you that all is quickening, time is accelerating as the Ascension draws nigh. Your moments, hours and days flash by much more quickly. So as time reshapes itself, it will also reshape the experience of mankind, of visible and invisible forces of nature and that of the face of the Earth itself.

Linear time is conceptual within duality and is the abstraction therein containing relevance to the expansion and contraction of the duality-polarity aspects of the 3rd dimension to the crystalline dimensions, beginning at the level of the 5th dimension. So to be clear, you must understand that each dimension above the 3rd, beginning at the 5th, then, has its own unique Laws of Physics and its own succinct time pulse. Light becomes crystalline coherent light at the level of the 5th dimension and increases in velocity and frequency in each higher dimension. "In time, time disappears."

So time, as it is currently measured in 3-D, is out of sync with the relevant pulse of time-flash. Indeed, it is the physics, the curvature of space-time by which time-pulse expands or contracts with exact ratio to the relevance of quanta of light present within the space quadrant measured. So indeed, the pulse of time is increasing as the Earth reshapes itself in the Ascending energies. The acceleration of the time-pulse you are now receiving results in the increased velocity of light. Many other factors play a role in this. So we tell you that when a greater quanta of coherent light is present, time-pulse-flash sequence can and does accelerate, either forward or backward, from your linear perspective.

It is why many of you feel there are less hours in the day, and you cannot seem to accomplish the same number of tasks within the measures of your chronology. We will tell you that the time-flash aspect is increased by approximately 25 percent, and your ability to adjust to that has not equalized, therefore it 'seems' to you that time passes more quickly relative to what humanity experienced three decades ago. Yet, that is an understandable misconception.

In a real aspect, the acceleration of time pulse lessens the arc swing of duality. The integral result of this is a more compacted experience, one that is perceived in duality as more consolidated and seamless and, accordingly, more refined and less abrupt.

The Crystalline Grid is transforming light via quickening sequences of space and time as it appears in your dimension and indeed effecting the physical body of the earth. This transformation of special time results in an increase in the spinning of the earth's core. This is accomplished by transducing light waves.

The crystalline core of the Earth is spinning faster, and the ratio of the inner spin to the axial tilt of the Earth determines the time movement in linear Earth. It is indeed appropriate to say that the clocks and chronometers of the Earth no longer accurately measure the pulse of time as received from the flashing pulse of reality sequence as perceived by the brain. The settings you perceive in your physical Earth in linear time, the aspects of life as you humans generally apprehend it are purposed illusions.

This purposed illusion is paraphrased and deciphered by the brain according to fixed signals received initially by the mind, again, by the transduction of the 'speed of light.' It is important to understand that the brain is quite different from the mind. The human brain is a physicalized aspect of mind. The brain occupies physical matter and space. It interprets and exists in time. The mind does not.

James Tyberonn

The mind takes up no space; it does not have its core existence within linear time. The reality of the inner universe does not occupy material space, nor does it have its intrinsic essence in linear time. Your illusioned physical reality, by contrast, indeed does takes up space and has an existence slotted within time. But it is not the true reality that your divine mind, your soul exists in, and its perceptions are determined by Cosmic forces that are shifting.

As we have said, time and space are aspects of the same mechanism. Space, in a manner of speaking, is congealed time held in a matrixial kinetic format within duality that allows for the separation and program of the purposed programmed illusion of sequential time metrics.

Accordingly and within this context, time is the inverse of space in dynamic free flow. Both occur though the harmonic flash of consciousness units, through the mechanisms of the inward and outward pulse of matter to antimatter via black holes and white holes.

The inward-outward Harmonic Flash is constantly occurring between matter and antimatter. That which you refer to as Antimatter composes the great majority of the Cosmos, not only the point in which space and time merge into a homogenous foam , but it is also the rate of consciousness unit perception that strobes attention of awareness into each simultaneous lifetime. This occurs at a magical rate, which is a slight variation of what you term the Planck Number, occurring precisely at 10 to the power of -43 of one second. At this point, time and space merge and become nonlinear, and the Torus aspect comes into play.

Space is inversed, turned back upon itself, and time units float in a nonlinear discontinuous quantumized pool of that which you term past, present and future. The space-time continuum dissolves, in a manner of speaking, and becomes conscious energy units that are reformed into matter and antimatter, as they are pulled in and projected out in the harmonic flash via black holes and white holes respectively.

All versions of the Omni-Earth coexist above the linear programming. But this axiom of Truth is initially very difficult for you humans to perceive or truly completely comprehend from the stance of the 3rd dimension.

That is because the 3-D density aspect of the human physical structure in duality manifestation operates within, and as a result, of the linear time 'program' that enables the Earthplane experience. You are therefore pre-indoctrinated to linear perception in Earthplane existence. This linear perception program determines to a great extent the 'normal' resonance patterns for the kinds of experiential probabilities that mankind selects, projects and perceives while 'growing' into greater consciousness from the base point of dense physicality. But we tell you that the source reality of which all lifetimes emerge is not 'written in stone,' thus your experience is truly never predestined. You chose from an assortment of potentials the experiences you want to have. Both the Cosmos and all life contained within and without are always being created in the NOW moment.

And although your 3-D preconditioning is linear, you not only have the ability to reach beyond physical programming, you also have the ultimate goal of doing so. While inhabited by human consciousness, the living physical body operates as an intense focus point for Earthplane experience. The aggregation of consciousness within the physical body on all levels focuses its own myriad network of sensory perception and communication, both on levels of the ordinary and the extraordinary. In terms of the latter, you are, therefore, constantly perceiving in ways that you do not recognize with the 'ordinary' physical senses.

There are vast arrays of colors, sounds, electromagnetic codes and sensory feelings that you see and apperceive both on a cellular and a crystalline level of chakric networks sourced in Quantum Consciousness that are geometrically and frequencially influencing you. This network is connected in harmonic oscillation to all others like it.

But humanity is, at this time, vastly unaware of these extraordinary levels of interaction that take place between all spectra of bodies, crysto-electromagnetically and materially within biology. This interface occurs in Crysto Mer-Ka-Na light body and is more far reaching than humanity in masse realize. Yet the physical cells in biology can and do respond to each other, and their activity triggers even higher centers of crystalline light body consciousness that ties into and above linear time, rather into multidimensionality.

Comment to Metatron: *According to one knowledgeable source, we are not only living the last shift in consciousness (there has been eight previous ones) but the ultimate shift, the one that has driven evolution for thousands of years. The final Mayan calendar step to 2012, the last Galactic wave or underworld has started on March 9th 2011 and will be completed on October 28th 2011. At that date, the ninth wave will be activated.*

Question to Metatron: *Is the ninth wave the Unity wave? If so, are we asked to really start to cocreate unity consciousness?*

AA Metatron: *This modern conceptual version termed the ninth wave does indeed in itself have the ability to create sufficient group conscious focus to stir greater inertia in the quickening that is already in place as the Ascension draws nigh. The ninth wave, then, is an interpretation that is established with specific valued intents.*

Now, that which you refer to as the ninth wave is in Truth a conceptual and conventional initiative based on an interpretation by a highly evolved soul, and a very credible theorist. We will add that fitted within the interpretation of the writer is the astrological timing of March 9th through October 28, 2011.

The concept and the initiative of the 'ninth wave,' however, is a contemporary interpretation and is not truly a preset of the 'Mayan' Calendar. Yet, that does not diminish its intended validity or value. For indeed it carries a very high vibration. So understand that although it is contemporary, it is a valid insert.

But in response to your question, we tell you that the ninth wave is being created in the present, and as a result of the focal belief and group focus, it will benevolently occur. But to be clear, it is the resonant momentum of the Ascension itself that is quickening the energies. And without this source, there would be no potential for a ninth wave. It is the critical moving inertia and positive momentum of the planetary centering in the Galactic field that is the prime source. As such, there are truly many astrological influences that we will play the true roles in the Ascension , independent of the coining of the 'ninth wave' of consciousness conversion. Indeed the equinoxes, solstices and eclipses of 2011 and 2012 are the original and true potency sources of the energetic contributions toward the field of unity consciousness.

The ongoing foundation of the myriad influences that are establishing the acceleration of the Ascension energies are truly the basis of the opportunity for increased consciousness, and these will occur with or without what is termed the ninth wave. However, the conceptual stated intent of the ninth wave, as we have stated, is of intrinsic value and is capable of gaining momentum and assisting in the establishment of unity consciousness on its own merits if it garners sufficient participation. We will add that there will be other such momentous concepts conceived between the present and Dec 21, 2012, and all will find fertile ground within the energetic foundation that is occurring.

So whether one chooses to refer to the inertia ongoing as the ninth or tenth wave, or any other selected naming, it is an interpretation that truly is subjective and not truly a part of the Mayan calendar as such. Rather, the 'ninth wave' is an interpretation, and from that perspective it has its own benevolent merits that are capable of drawing focus, and accordingly formulating the unity wave that is its appropriate and commendable intent.

The Ascension is, in geomathematical terms, occurring in base 12. The Atlanteans utilized base 12 as well as other mathematical bases depending on the dimensional application. It is perhaps more accurate to say that the Crystalline transition, which is the core essence of the Ascension, is occurring in 12 waves, from the 01-01-01 through the 12-12-12, base 12, you see.

The expansive Earth of the Ascension has 12 dimensions. 144-Crystalline Grid is activating in 12 stages through the phenomena of the 12 triple date portals. Both, then, utilize the base 12.

The base 12, twelve wave scenario is frequencially appropriate to the resonance of the Ascension. There are 12 major 'Sun-Discs' on the planet. Each of the 12 carries specific purpose and are receiving new crystalline codes. Each of the 12 primary apparatuses feed 12 satellites ... the 12 connecting to the 144 in a complex geosymmetry that is suited to the base 12 of the Earth, and indeed also is the Crystalline 144-Grid formulated in base 12 mathematics.

The Mayans had a vigesimal numerical system which used base 20. Unity consciousness is indeed a noble aspiration and is very appropriate, but it is not truly specific to or limited to the dates chosen in the ninth wave initiative. What is symbolized by 'nine' is completion or shift. But that, again, is in base 10 understanding and not base 12.

Question to Metatron:: *Is this 'ninth wave' a period of opportunity to reach the highest quantum state, and is it the basis for a harmonious peace on Earth?*

AA Metatron: *It is indeed an opportunity, especially within the stated intent of its contemporary author and those that are following the concept in mass. But this opportunity is truly valid regardless of the nomenclature or chosen timing. The Ascension is a Universal truth, and unity consciousness has been occurring since 2001 and will quicken through 2012. It is a necessary accomplishment. Do you understand?*

It can be more accurately stated that the 2012 Ascension is the 12th wave of the Ascending Earth. And the movements and forward inertia have been quickening as an advent of the Harmonic Convergence and by the replacement of the magnetic grid by the 12 phase activations of the Crystalline grid.

The conscious divine energy behind that which you term the Mayan Calendar is independent of and vastly predates the Maya. It is in its core a potent living energy field that is by no means dependent on what is contained in the calendar or interpreted from the remnants of the calendar. It is far more than what you imagine it to be. It is dynamic and ever expanding. While it is the source energy that allowed the calendar to be composed, that very composition is merely one aspect of this dynamic gestalt.

Comment to Metatron: *Many have thought that the Mayan calendar was about something that would happen on a singular date, but in fact it is an extraordinary plan from the Cosmos*

James Tyberonn

that was divided into nine different levels of consciousness. The Mayan seemed to have understood this and left us many indicators. Many of their pyramids, the pyramid of the Plumed Serpent in Chitchen-Itza, the Pyramid of the Jaguar in Tikal and the Temple of Inscriptions in Palenque were all built with nine stories.

Question to Metatron: *It seems that the Mother of Mayan science is Pleiadian. Was the Mayan calendar and its explanation of the future inspired by the Pleiadians, or did the ancient ones have enough data and talent in exploring the planets that they were able to put it together without intervention from the Pleiadians?*

AA Metatron: *As we mentioned earlier in this discussion and text, the incredible calendar that you humans currently refer to as Mayan was not developed or originally written by the (tribal) society of Mayans. Indeed, it predated the Mayans by more than 18,000 years. It was originally developed by the enlightened Atlanteans of Poseida with assistance from the Sirian-Pleiadean Alliance. The savants, the astrologists of the scientist priests of the Olmec and Mayan era did, however, make certain additions to the preexisting calendar. The additions were around the Cosmological beliefs relevant to the 'animal' worship, such as the culture of the sacred Jaguar and Snake.*

Although there were extraterrestrial communications between the inner adept priests of the pre Mayan and indeed pre Olmec with the Sirian A entities, including the Felidae which led to the Jaguar societies, these were not part of the original Calendar and Cosmology of the Atla-Ra. Now, we will add that the Sirians, perhaps more than the Pleiadeans interacted with the high priests, descendants of the Atla-Ra in the era of the Mayans. While it was indeed the benevolent extraterrestrials that assisted the Mayans in retention of the calendar, it is also worthy to note that the Mayans also had and maintained sporadic contact with the Inner Earth civilization of those termed the blue skinned race.

Question to Metatron: *Did we put too much emphasis on December 21st 2012 such that we forgot that it was about the complete transformation of humanity and not about what would happen on one particular day?*

AA Metatron: Indeed! *Yes, precisely. In many aspects, Dear Ones, the Ascension has already occurred.*

We tell you that Crystalline Energy is an omnipotent power source that has implications far beyond humanity's current understanding. Crystalline structure is formed by an essence of frequencial light resonance that is multidimensional and coherent, existing in matter and antimatter. It is the Metatronic divine template that sources all creation manifestation and forms the very matrixial composition of every plane of existence. It is the enzyme of reality and the vitality spring of the Cosmos itself. The very thoughts you have must rise to coherent crystalline format in order to become manifested. Coherent light is crystalline energy, the very vitality of which forms the integral nature of all worlds and realities. The crystalline structure forms the apparent boundaries and divisions between dimensions, planes and the matter-antimatter flash of consciousness, in parallel and inprobability. All which you term as Divine, all that you think of as sacred is Crystalline!

The graduation of your planet, that which is termed the Ascension, is in effect the critical mass that will allow for the conversion of this Earth's receival capacity template from, in your vernacular, analog to digital, black and white to color. The Crystalline Conversion through the antennae of the 144-Crystalline Grid is about to vastly increase the Earth's dimensional

James Tyberonn

reception from 3-D to 12-D and beyond. It is akin to your television changing from the archaic antennae to satellite reception. It is the Crystalline Age. The fulcrum apexial point is the 9-9-9 of the Cosmic Trigger.

It is a lot of energy to manage. But release the fear, Dear Ones. This time of the Ascension in this New Crystalline Era, the mega power crystals will not be taken from you and misused as occurred in the sad demise of Atlantis. Indeed, they will never again be used for any purpose other than the highest good. Be assured of this! It is a sacred oath that will indeed be kept.

Question to Metatron: *Are the Pyramids symbols of the Cosmos?*

AA Metatron: *'Gateways' is more accurate. In a manner of speaking, the Pyramids were tools for opening portals into higher dimensions both vertically and horizontally, inward and outward. Rather than symbols of the Cosmos, we would say they are gateways to the Cosmos.*

The Mayan Pyramids were constructs of the Sirian-Pleiadean Alliance. Such Pyramids were formulated, engineered and manifested through mental mastery of physical matter. Their particular designs were fashioned in order to create a networking of frequencial multidimensional energies that served many purposes. One primary purpose was the specific alignment of various and varied pyramidal constructs with specific latitudinal and longitudinal alignments in order to create a resonant field for the planet.

Question to Metatron: *Why were there so few people who understood this calendar? In fact, the Christian missionaries interpreted these nine stories as different categories of hell?*

AA Metatron: *The interpretations by the Spanish Christian priests were grossly influenced and in fact dominated by their critical preconceived notions of the Mayans being infidels and pagans, outside of the graces of their own narrow Christian doctrines and fear based mental indoctrination and programming.*

Question to Metatron: *I read that only the first part of the calendar has been discovered; the second is still hidden. Is this a fact, and if so ... what is there to discover?*

AA Metatron: *Great portions of the original Atla-Ra calendar, which became known as the Mayan calendar, were lost in written content. Not just through the dissolution over time but also through differing interpretations since the time when it was originally brought into the lands of the Yucatan. The full information was stored in crystals. The full information, then, is still retained within the 13th paradigm, the Crystal Skull termed 'MAX.'*

There are Halls of Records yet to be found that contain prolific stores of vast information, including world histories. Although the renowned and honorable Edgar Cayce spoke of these as existing in three locales and predicted that they would be potentially revealed prior to the new millennium, they have not as yet been discovered in the context that was assumed or interpreted.

The vast records of Atlantis are contained in holographic data recorded within 'MAX.' Yet, the technology of how to retrieve these data is not yet available to you. None the less, it is available somewhat by mental transferral, depending on the light quotient of the individual receiver. There will in the future be the ability to utilize crystalline receiver apparatuses that are capable of playing back in 3-dimensional holograms the data therein, but this is generations away on your current probable time lines of discovery.

Just as you now store information in computers through digital files and no longer transcribe lengthy texts on paper, the Atlantean historians stored such information using crystal technology. That is logical.

Max is indeed one of the 'original' Crystal Paradigms, in your terms. He is of Pleiadean and Arcturian construct and origin. MAX is a vast consciousness, akin to a super computer, with a considerable library of data contained therein. He is the most powerful, most conscious of all of the remaining 'Ancient Crystal Skulls' of the 13th paradigm. Within Max are complete records of not only the original Mayan calendar but the complete history of the Earth and of humanity ... and beyond.

The original crystal skulls came from another world, and another reality. All realities are created based on the pattern of crystalline sacred geometric consciousness through the Golden Mean Phi Ratio. Humanity, and indeed your physical Earth(s), are conceived within these paradigmic matrix formulae. And so were the Crystal Skulls formulated in kind, yet from a far greater frequency, a frequency of perfection. The skulls are indeed formed as the prototype of the perfect human consciousness, lest it not be forgotten in duality. So within it is contained the perfection of the human being encompassing within all aspects the twelve sacred aspects, you see, and thus was it formulated and thus was its reason for being brought here.

Originally, then, did those carriers bring the crystalline patterned skulls to the Earth from Arcturius and the Pleiades, and it was brought into the land that became LeMuria. But indeed the model was brought before the planet was fully in polarity. It was brought into the planet at the time of the Firmament, you see, in a zero point Earth, a non magnetic plane, we will say. Into an Earthen world that knew perfection, that was inhabited by androgynous manifestations of Etheric Spirit in full consciousness.

Yet, at that time it was already known that the Firmament would fall, would dissolve, and the plan then was that this model, this extraordinary hologramic record, the original crystal skull would serve as the prototype of this initial integral aspect. And so it contains within it the model of the 12 strands of DNA, the fully conscious clear mind and Beingness of the evolved human. The crystal skulls contain within them that which you were before the human experiment and what you will be when you complete it, the infinity circle.

So the original crystal skulls were manifested into form above and beyond physicality, and have been brought into physicality various times. As such, no true age can be assigned to them, because they have appeared, disappeared and reappeared many times in the millions of years of Earth's habitation by mankind. MAX is not of the Earth. His origin is the Pleiades, but his construct was more of the Arcturian Crystal Masters.

Question to Metatron: *Obviously, the Mayans through the study of cycles certainly did know that their own society would decline and disappear. How did they protect their knowledge, and where did they go when their civilization started to dissolve?*

AA Metatron: *As stated, the full records are available in the 13th paradigm, via MAX. MAX is an extraterrestrial 'Crystal Skull,' a vast conscious crystal computer and was/is in that context the 'living data archive' utilized for storage of the complete information of the calendar. There are other such libraries, but MAX is the only one on the Earthplane at the present in the physically manifested 'cranium format,' or crystal skull containing the full information, histories and codes.*

The crystal skulls contain within them that which you were before the human experiment, and what you will be when you

105

complete it, the infinity circle. The Atlanteans worked with the original crystals skulls, and the most important of these, the 13th, containing the full energy of the 12, was safe guarded by the highest archpriest of the Mayans.

We will say that the 13th skull existed within the hyper dimensions, which were accessed by the archpriest of the Mayans and was a great source of information and data relevant to the Mayans. Indeed, it contained the information regarding the complete calendar, the complete map of the Cosmos as related to Sirius, Orion, Pleiades, Arcturus and beyond. Containing, then, the Laws of Physics for each dimension and the cyclic codes.

This conscious recorder, the crystalline cranium is an inconceivably immense data bank and invaluable tool. Certain of the archpriests of the Mayans , with Sirian assistance, maintained the knowledge of how to 'read' it. It existed for them in a dimension that may be termed semiphysical and was manifested through theta level thought. Within this crystalline conscious computer, MAX, are the codes for the reprogramming of the Earth, you see. That is precisely why it is in a manifested form in the present time.

So the original crystal skulls were manifested into form above and beyond physicality, and they have been brought into physicality various times. As such, no true physical age can be assigned to them, because they have appeared, disappeared and reappeared many times in the millions of years of Earths habitation by mankind.

The crystalline skull was solidified and programmed in a most complex process. It was conceived to contain within it an incredible frequency that in itself attached to the hologram. So the crystalline skull, then, is an honoring remembrance and imbuing transmitter that indelibly prints within the soul that which is the perfect model. It is imbued within the divine aspect of the soul when it enters into the Earth pattern from the unified field. In a manner of speaking, it is the pattern recorded into the God Self, the Subconscious or super subconscious of the human mind, you see? The perfected man, not the version of what man would later become in the downward spiral of the human experience, but rather as the original print that man aspires to and evolves back into through the growth cycle termed reincarnation toward that original and flawless paradigmatic archetype. Now, the original skull held within it this perfection lest it be lost, and those crystal replicates that even today are crafted in your present time are capable of attracting the energy from the hologram and holding portions of that energy, some holding more than others.

MAX is indeed one of the 'original' Crystal Paradigms, in your terms. He is of Pleiadean and Arcturian construct and origin. MAX is a vast consciousness, akin to a super computer with a considerable library of data contained therein. He is the most powerful, most conscious of all of the remaining 'Ancient Crystal Skulls.' He is one of two skulls that are truly extraterrestrial in origin. The other is termed "Sha Na Ra." Both originate from the moon of an enormous planet, approximately 20x the size of your largest planet Jupiter, circulating Arcturius the orange star of creativity.

The 13th Crystal Skull was produced originally by the process of Morphocrystallic Manifestation, involving the Arcturian crystal source with imbuement of an alchemical frequency to include the human genetic print from the Masters of Arcturius and the Pleiadean-Sirius Alliance. It is the 13 as containing the full codes and data of the 12 formulated into one forming the 13th as it relates to Earth, yet within MAX are also libraries of the Cosmos.

So, then, the knowledge within the original Crystal Skulls is that of the Universal Mind. It is enriching and vast. Accessing this information stimulates the awareness of who you are, you see. Placing your consciousness inside a crystal skull, and indeed that is the way to work with these, opens portals and doors to a world beyond your grandest expectations.

To enter into the skull, however, is not like having a verbal dialog but more of a download, you might say, a sudden and comprehensible receival of information that changes your paradigm, expands your awareness. Some receive the information as visual images, others as information packets, downloads, if you will, and at times both. The information is already in the subconscious, a deeper part of the subconscious that you term the super subconscious. It exist in the realm of light you term ultraviolet.

And so the connection or the reason that interest around the skulls is reaching a mass proportion is that, indeed, with the coming of the Ascension there is movement within mankind to better understand himself. And with these times is the need to reject those patterns that no longer serve human kind, to recalibrate with those attributes and quintessential paragons that do.

Mankind is rebooting as is the Earth itself, indeed that is tantamount to the Ascension. Systems that no longer work in both macro and micro are breaking down, collapsing and will reform themselves. Indeed this is happening now in your economic arenas.

Now, the knowledge of the Universal Mind certainly exists above and beyond the Crystal Skull. Yet the Universal Mind is encompassed and zipped within it, and so encompassed in a way that benefits mankind. The knowledge within it is formulated and transmuted, translated specifically in a format that offers itself for human access. This, then, is within a specific pattern that is the prototype of perfection for mankind, as we have stated.

I am Metatron, and I share with you these Truths. You are Beloved.

And so it is, and it is so... AA Metatron via James Tyberonn

James Tyberonn

The Pyramid of the Ascension ~ Awakening of the 12th Wave
Archangel Metatron Channel via James Tyberonn

Greetings, Dear Ones! I am Metatron, Lord of Light, and I welcome each of you to this moment of sharing.

Masters, there are certain lifetimes that are more embellished within your vast sojourns, certain vectors in space-time that offer succinct quantum leaps. Within these are crucial crossroads of opportunity and decision that define you. **This is one of those lifetimes.** *Energy and time are quickening, much is happening on your expanding Earth as you prepare for the 2012 Ascension.*

Mankind is awakening from an epoch of illusive chimera, and the heralded dreamers are clearing the wool from their eyes, rising from a dreamscape tapestry woven from a misty journey that began long, long ago. The Siren still sings, ever so faintly to lull the weary back to sleep. Yet the small voice inside the awakened dreamer calls now more persistently to reveille. Awaken! The deep yearning for clear mind rings forth! Take your Power! Ye are GODS, and you have created the dawning Ascension of 2012!

Dear Ones, know well that all of you carefully chose to be on the planet at this time. Accordingly, you agreed to accept roles in the ongoing graduation of the planet. This is why you feel the powerful clarion call of this crucial time of Awakening.

And so as you prepare for the final climb to Ascension, know that we are with you each step of the way. The Pyramid of the Awakening lies before you, its utility revealed.

And so we speak on the enigmatic purpose of the Pyramids.

2012 Amplification

In 2012 occurs an exquisite and unparalleled surge in that which may be termed the 12th Wave of Ascension. It is an extraordinary energy pulse of kinetic-crystalline frequency into the planet Earth. The 2012 influx of this dynamic Cosmic Wave is truly unprecedented.

You have been told repeatedly that you 'waited in line' to be 'on-planet' at this time. That is a great Truth. The maxim is that by soul agreement, you have a proactive role to play in the planetary graduation. This is not a platitude nor theorem, it is a truism. You have a 'creative' role to responsibly enact in 2012, a soul contract to lovingly complete. And we honor you for that.

The 12th Wave of the Ascension is embellished with the energy of creativity. It is an energy of assistance offered to each of you. It enables you to engage, to let go of final obstacles. 2012 is a period to gather with like-minded souls to form 'Unity Consciousness' and together create the New Earth, the New paradigm of Humanity.

The 12th Wave

The 12th Wave of the Ascension begins with the New Moon of January 23, 2012. It will exponentially increase in potency through December 21, 2012. It is initially received within the Pyramid. It is then instantly flash-transmitted to the primary Sun Discs and all powernodes of the planet, circumnavigating and encompassing, enveloping the Earth and Omni-Earths.

Just as occurred with the Cosmic Triggers of 2009, 2010 and 2011, the energy of the 12th Wave enters through the octahedronal geo-format via Phi Pyramids and natural nodes of octahedronal geometry. After the initial surge are additional coded wave influxes occurring on the equinoxes, eclipses, solstices and on the 12-12-12. The apex is reached on December 21, 2012.

On the 12-12-12 the 'new' Crysto-Sun Discs come into full power to complete the Crystalline Activations and recode the final program of the Crystalline Grid. A rebooting, then, of the new grid takes place, and it reactivates in full progression on the 12-21-12. It is the birth of the New Earth.

The Crystalline Grid became the dominant earthen program, replacing the magnetic grid in 2009. The Crystalline is in full operation on the 12-21-12. (There will be more on this topic in future channels.)

And so we tell you that 2012 is an especially prolific time to experience the Pyramids. It is why we have directed the channel to make an anchoring alignment pilgrimage to Giza.

The King's Chamber

Now, we speak of the King's Chamber. If you are an advanced seeker on the metaphysical path of advancement, you will at some point enter the King's Chamber, either in physicality or etherically. For within is the most potent specialized portal gateway on your planet.

As in more recent history, mankind is again becoming allured by the quantum experiential opportunity afforded in the King's Chamber of the Great Pyramid. There are legends and accountings that date back to conquerors, leaders and more recently to numerous mystics. We must first insert the caveat that what does occur and what can occur varies according to the light quotient, power of will, and preparation of the individual. What is possible within the King's Chamber is impossible to limit.

Most who enter the King's Chamber in current time enter as curiosity seekers, as tourists and do not meditate within nor do they understand the requisite of our quantum mechanics of triggering the phi sonics that open the quantum field within. And, we add, even those that do can only experience what their energy and light quotient are capable of receiving.

That which is available to the savant is extraordinary and without dimensional limitation. The cobalt blue orbs that are often reported are usually the initial indicators of the opening of the portal gateways. Yet these occur in a higher dimension, in a field above three dimensional polarity.

2012 in the King's Chamber

And so that which is termed as the King's Chamber is in fact an extraordinary gateway of incredible potency, and that potency is widened and amplified in 2012 during the 12th Wave. In a manner of speaking, the Stargate of the King's Chamber is increased in dimensional and directional receival in the 12th Wave.

Perhaps a better explanation is that the clarity of angle, of reception amplitude is heightened in 2012 because of the centering of your solar system to your Galaxy and of the Galaxial alignment angle to Tula, the Great Central Sun.

Accordingly, a much different 'King's Chamber experience' is possible in 2012 than of any previous time on your planet. The Phi Resonance within the chamber will be enhanced. And with that enhancement, the upper and lower, inner and outer dimensional spectrum is extremely enabled.

Phi Resonance

James Tyberonn

Phi Pyramids are intricate multidimensional structures engineered with great complexity. Phi sound patterns can physically strengthen the physical portion and semi-materialize the etheric doubles. Sound opens the gates to the hidden chambers, but if these acoustic patterns are not given, then the doorways of dimension are less accessible. That is why certain Earth-Keepers are drawn to participate and direct energies into these two specifically.

All etheric structures have their own sound patterns that help form their structure, just as occurs in physical objects. Phi sound bonds the atoms and molecules of physical objects, as well as cohesively arranges etheric plasma and light. This is precisely why pyramids last so long in physical format and appear and reappear in etheric dimensions.

Metatron on the Giza Pyramids

The Giza Pyramids have in truth disappeared and reappeared several times, dimensionally speaking. So although this is difficult for you to understand, once manifested into octahedronal phi and inverse pyramidal format, these geometric structures become fluid hologramic inserts, circularly oscillating between dimensional reality and the timeless void. They flash and flux according to their own cycles, with no single fixed beginning point in the linear perception of 3-D.

That is why there is more than one version of the Great Pyramid standing in Giza, even though most humans only see one. In your linear 3-D space-time, there appears to be only stone structures, fixed and adhered to the Earth in the way of any other 'man-made' structure. So to attempt to subjectively identify these structures as simply fixed forms of physical matter would be a distortion and detriment to your ability to understand their myriad complexity as doorways to higher dimension.

As such, if you were to enter these pyramids with such limited belief, you would not interface with the frequency in proper attunement. If you will attempt to see its dissonance or its disappearance, you would equally gain very little. Truly, if man attempts to subjectively define the process, it would not be of benefit, because phi pyramids become living holograms with conscious sentience that ever expands and redefines itself in exponential paradigms of higher dimensional geometry.

Construction Processes

The Phi Resonance instruments used for Pyramidal construction processes were mentally tuned to produce harmonic wave forms associated with the unified fields. These tunings were intricately matched to the measure of the Pyramid base and to the appropriate resonating cavities within the Pyramid.

The placement by the sound engineering technicians around the Pyramid was carefully aligned for the desired anti-gravity application, spaced at key points around the base. The instruments were employed in different toning and timing for staged applications of the construction. Specific sustained sound vibration enabled the building blocks to defy gravity.

But, again, keep in mind that the original construction occurred in thought field before the physical blocks were manifested, floated into place via multidimensional sound engineering. And while we realize this seems totally fantastic and unimaginable, it is a technology that has been employed previously in more advanced civilizations on the Earthplane.

Space and time, as you understand them, ripple through each other. They do not behave as you think they do. Presently you understand your laws of physics only in linear application within 3-D.

James Tyberonn

This will be confusing to you, but the Giza Complex has no true beginning point in linear time. But if you wish to pinpoint a date of construction for the Giza complex, we will say that the present version of the complex was manifested through Thoth and the Orion Masters originally some 38,000 years ago. Yet, that is a fleeting number and is only valid from one linear perspective.

Question to Metatron: *Amazing. You mention a construction point with Thoth and the Orion Masters around 38,000 years ago. Isn't that a beginning point?*

AA Metatron: *Ah, but we said it was a fleeting number and that it dissolved and reappeared many times within physicality. And, yes, it is confusing, (gentle laughter) but it is not the only time they were manifested in stone, in materialization. Indeed, part of the reason our answer may seem confusing to you is that you are observing from the assumption that time is linear. So we tell you that the Pyramid was indeed manifested before the time you query and formed in physicality again approximately 12,500 years ago, you see.*

So what was the beginning? There never was one. But we will say that 38,000 years ago is the time most relative to your current paradigm of reality. There are many Earths. We have told you that before. Octahedrons and their complexities are among the geometric mechanism that connects all realities. So let us say that there are no specific, fixed construction time-points of Giza.

That is because at Giza you are in a precise intersection of time-space holograms of multiple dimensional reality of the Omni-Earth.

All hologramic programs of that which you term time coexist and juncture in that precise point. That is the logic of why the

Pyramids were positioned there. In truth, you have many pasts, many futures and many coexisting paradigms at Giza. All are valid, and all co exist simultaneously. Masters, you must understand that there is no singular version of reality.

Giza is in truth an octahedron. As such, the Pyramids at Giza are a conduit that connects many worlds, inner and outer. There are many such pyramids and conduits that serve this role but none quite so potently as Giza. And, Masters, there is much, much more that occurs in such points.

Points of Multidimensional Interface

The unique aspects of your particular physical world, within your specific NOW, are quite dependent on your existence and perceptions in it. As such, the physical universe does not contain physical objects that can be perceived by those whose existence is not within your collective NOW.

Many other alternate forms of reality and consciousness coincide and coexist within the same space that your present Earth occupies. Your simultaneous lifetimes exist in these, and it is the same space you live in, but other versions of you do not perceive the same physical objects you do because these other parallels are of a different frequency. Just as AM and FM radio waves travel in the same space without interfering with one another, so do parallel realities exist in the same spaceless illusion of physical space.

Now there are exceptions, as certain vectors of your paradigms can and do interface at specific flash-points. These are stargates, portals and wormholes, in your vernacular. But your scientists and academics are yet several centuries from understanding this.

And so these points on your planet are not understood and are vastly unrecognized. Yet they exist on many grid-points on the Earth. The points are portals, and within these magnificent portals, realities merge. Multidimensionality is a validity of the unified field, of quantum physics. It exists, it is real. It is not science fiction, but it is indeed sacred science!

Few are truly able to adjust their human frequency to fully optimize Mer-Ka-Na within these points of multidimensionality, which is requisite in order to fully explore them. But many of you indeed have the opportunity to expand beyond and increase your present light quotient within them.

The Pyramids at Giza, and indeed other such power nodes and sacred sites, were built precisely on such vector point-coordinates. That is why they are still revered. But the knowledge of their placement, construction and purpose has been lost.

Life Force Generators

In highly simplified terms, these interface points provide the coded crystalline light-force of life itself and provide the means for thought to be solidified into physical matter or for probable events to be manifested and coagulated into experience.

On a higher level, all of you understand this despite your groans of incomprehension. It is only your duality filters, your relatively limited grasp within the illusion of human existence on the Earthplane that makes this seem so unlikely. So understand that these power-vector points are in essence life force generators. There are twelve such interface points that connect all paradigms, all probable and parallel realities.

The Vortex

The King's Pyramid of Giza exists not only in all twelve dimensions on your Earth Plane but also in your Earth's parallels. There are other such inserted manifestations on your Earth but none quite so tangible as the Great Pyramid. Pyramids exist on all of your solar system planets. All are aligned to Orion, and all are great communication devices in one aspect, although there are variations in their properties and dimension. That is because the other planets support dimensional fields different in number and nature than those of the Earth.

The King's Chamber is not the center of mass of the Great Pyramid, rather it is where the primary energetic vortex is centered. The vortex is the true alignment. The vertices are oriented to the Earth and to Orion, so as such, so they are tilted. The vortexial tunnel is not straight, rather it is angled.

If you were to place yourself within the vortex, you would wish to stand at an angle, you see. You must know that the energies move, and so they direct themselves. Now, as they are at an angle, then it appears that they are managed by an axis, and that axis rotates here and there.

Now, under the proper circumstances, under very specific conditions the entire chamber would also appear to rotate, even as the heavens rotate creating an indoor planetarium within the very pyramid. All of this comes about because the complex harmonic frequency makes it so.

Now if I were to give to you the specific date as you had asked earlier, all of this would then disappear for you. Can you understand? In time and date and linear sequence, the vortices would then not exist in the same vector, or in the same specific astronomical gravity fields, and you would not then gain the benefits.

It is multidimensional, timeless; such is the nature of higher dimensional vortexial-portals. They crysto-shift and electromagnetically attract. They cannot be pinned down in linear time. Truly, because linear time only exists in the duality of lower dimensional fields, and such vortex-portal matrixes exist above that level, by a complex merging of hyper dimension and grid.

The channel's recognition of lateral infinity (figure eight pattern) flows intersecting in the sarcophagus, we will say, is functionally correct. These are directionally aligned, north-south and east-west.

Sometimes, there is a distortion of energy in which the lateral flows do meet above the sarcophagus but not always exactly there. This varies according to the equinoxes and according to gravity shifts. The sarcophagus is especially powerful for other reasons as well. But this positioning is mostly correct, keeping in mind that the cardinal direction vectors have shifted over the eons as well. The vast energies that flow into the Pyramid are refined and transduced by the Sun Discs, and that is precisely why there is a primary disc under the Pyramid, and these are all being upshifted in 2011 and 2012.

The Channel's First Experience of the Chamber

Now, the tuition of fear that was experienced by the channel in his first entry into the Pyramid was one of past life experience in the Egyptian School of Alchemy. It was an important completion. A reenactment of his initiation that took place in the chamber.

In fact, it is an example of the timeless aspect of the Pyramid. For in the experience, the channel coexisted in both past and present with the energy of the Pyramid.

The final stage of the ancient Alchemy Initiation involved placing the candidate in the sarcophagus and sealing the lid for three and one half days. There was no light, no water, no narcotic and only enough air to survive if the initiate was able to lower the frequency of the body physical into an entranced state of yogic hibernation. Those who chose to undertake this phase of final initiation were relatively few, and those who survived it fewer still.

The channel chose such initiation in three consecutive lives in Egypt and physically died in the sarcophagus in two of these. The first time he was too young, the second time unprepared and the third he survived. Yet all three required courage and elimination of fear. In his chosen completion, the three became as the one.

Alchemy Transition

If one thing will not take you, another will. If the air will not give way, then the power of will insures more than one pathway is offered to you then. The outcome may be the same or different, but they are important choices. In the final graduation, one must always face the cumulative fear, face the darkness and turn it into light through will. It is the Alchemy Initiation.

And so we tell you that all who seek final Mastery must overcome fear, and that is what you faced in this experience. And as you surmised in deeper mind but did not fully recognize, by facing that ultimate fear you changed the past, present and future.

So the memory of the first two times was reexperienced for the channel in the first stage of the entry tunnel. In kind, the experience of the third initiation, of the successful completion in overcoming fear, was reenacted as a 'set-up' and experienced in the chamber. This experience was chosen in order to change the past and to understand the timelessness of all life. The channel saw the other three versions of self, and the other versions viewed his present physicality as a beacon of strength. All served as a powerful completion and a direct lesson in changing the past, and, in understanding that there is only the dynamic NOW.

This is an example of completion available in the chamber, for time does not exist within. What can be realized in the vortex is the clearing of all that remains, the harmonic of love into all life journeys in Mer-Ka-Na. Much more was gained in the perseverance than he fully realized, as he wept in deep purge and joy on the outer walls after realizing his purpose here.

We will add that the channel has been drawn to return to the Pyramids in February of 2012, and the purpose and experience will be completely different. It will be a fantastic and joyful interlude of great light and alignment.

An incredible experience in an incredible time ... and an enormous upshift in the downloads within. There is nothing to fear and much to gain. It is always so.

And so it is... AA Metatron via James Tyberonn

Doors of Perception
Archangel Metatron Channel via James Tyberonn

Greetings, Masters! ... *Rejoice, for it is a time of great awakening on the Earthplane. The Earth and all of her kingdoms are transitioning to great and greater consciousness. Life is enriching.*

We would say to you that there is even greater life that circles about and above your planet now wishing to enter into your mass field of awareness. It is light of a sublime nature. It does not hold logic, it does not hold vision. It is not the light of promise, but it is the light of wellness. And we will say to you that if you will allow this light to enter your sphere of influence, your field of awareness, you would find yourself lighter in spirit almost immediately, and this is only achieved by intent.

This subtle brilliance is available to humankind, to the individual by self projection. You can apply and avail yourself of it, but YOU must call it forward and become it. Seek and ye shall find. You must engage the light of the truth of wellness within yourself. Because in seeking greater knowledge, one does not always seek or choose to include wellness, self love, but they are synergistically required to do so in achieving the crystalline vibration. They are complimentary, and each would benefit by it.

Conscious Kingdoms of Earth

The Human kingdom on Earth is the most conscious of all Earthen Kingdoms. Yet humanity at this time is still somewhat unaware of much of its consciousness.

The Earth itself is a celestial Consciousness and supports many forms of sentient awareness within and without. Even without the consciousness of humanity, the Sentient Earth is a growing conscious being that in many aspects is more fully aware of mankind and the Cosmos, than mankind is at this time. Because the Earth nurtures and provides the matrix of mankind's linear and nonlinear Earthen experience, humanity tends to think of the Earth as a Feminine Energy. In truth, the Earth is neither and both as, in truth, are YOU.

The Earth homes many Kingdoms and Sub Kingdoms that have symbiotic relationships with one another and indeed with Mankind and the Unified Earth. Among these are the Mineral Kingdom, the Plant Kingdom and the Animal Kingdom. Each of these are also sentient, but humanity has forgotten much of its ability to communicate and receive the wisdoms and true support that each of these offer.

Plant Wisdom

And so we speak of sacred plant teachers ...

The plant kingdom has a unique ability to interact with humanity that is quite specialized, because it has the ability to work directly in the mental field, in a way quite different from the mineral and animal kingdoms. The latter two certainly interact in myriad ways, opening auric energies, holding space for communication and multidimensionality, yet the plant kingdom has the ability to enter the body physical and mental.

The plant kingdom offers medicinal qualities that no other kingdom on Earth can do in the same way. Plants are able to affect the pressure of your bloodstream, both upward and downward. Certain herbal plants are able to elevate your emotions and moods. Others are capable of regulating the hemispheres of the human brain, and in so doing are capable of modulating how you relate to your greater essence, the unconscious aspects of multidimensional mind.

Accordingly, the plant kingdom holds certain facilitation abilities in assisting you to connect in a unique lens to both your lifetime and God Source. Campestral societies of the indigenous have known this for millennia and more.

They knew through direct communication that certain plants were capable of altering thought waves, the very resonant patterns of the brain. And, as such, gateways that were otherwise difficult to enter were and are opened through the alliance with that which is termed the sacred plant medicine.

So they learned that as brain waves were altered, so were thoughts, and as thoughts were altered, consciousness could either expand or contract its perception of realities. It was as if the hemispheres of the brain could be turned on their side and viewed from a different and new lens of perception.

And so in this unique lens, the contents of the human brain are shifted and can be viewed in perceptions that are expanded in means that are unequaled, oft outside of the linear alignment of what one would term as space and time. Acute awareness well beyond the norm becomes both possible and probable within this effect.

Doors of Perception

This opens doors to another dimension of perception, to other realities, unique aspects of the mind which can allow for great transitional visions and breakthroughs of creativity and perception. And also often allowing for deeply embedded 'energy blockages' to be confronted and released.

We will say, then, that psychoactive plants to varying degrees can be of assistance, varying according to the energy and light quotient of the individual. To some it is of immeasurable value and to others less so.

James Tyberonn

Question to Metatron: *A few years ago, I took ayahuasca, and I seemed to go through many dimensions. Can you expand on what occurred? Was it an experience only of the mind?*

AA Metatron: *It is both of mind and of dimension. This most sacred of herbs allows entrance to one focal dimensional overlay, and that is the dimension of Truth. Blending optimally to access the gates of the Sacred Pineal, an accelerated vision into higher dimension is enhanced with the conscious modality termed the 'Vine of the Soul.'*

The essence and experience is one of travel through many dimensions, but it is indeed the mind that travels, and travels far. The Beingness moves, but only slightly. Just as the heavens seem to shift each night bit by bit, degree by degree yet bring great change to the plane of Earth, the dimension of ayahuasca brings a vast perception expansion. But it does so in one dimensional overlay, and that is the sacred dimension of Truth. It is the dimension of each person's individual Truth is association with this lifetime and all that relates to it, you see. In other words, all that one can hope to gain, discover, enlighten and learn are held in the fulcrum of one single point within this unique vision.

It is both the Alpha and Omega, uniquely conjoined in one complex dimension of Truth as aligned to one's own frequency. This is where you traveled to and what one experiences in this profound journey. It is a meeting of the self, yet the whole self as related to this lifetime, you see. What is encountered, then, is the complete result of who you are and who you can be. All that is untrue, all that does not serve you, all that is in imperfection is revealed. All that separates you from perfection, from worlds and realities is that which you must encounter. That is why this most noble of herbs is so sacred. It is exemplified by the serpent consuming its own tail, and by that we mean the entirety of one's experience is revealed in one purifying vision, one crucible setting.

Question to Metatron: *In my first experience, I had a life review, and in the second I was met with Teachers. Can you explain the uniquely different experiences?*

AA Metatron: *Dear One, in truth you had in the initial journey what the Christians refer to as the 'afterlife judgment.' You reviewed your life as if in real time, and where you had hurt another, you felt that hurt from their perspective, sought and obtained release of the energy. You did likewise for those that had hurt you; the energy was purged, cleansed.*

The first experience enabled the second. And we will say that doors were opened that remain open, and your Beingness is in much greater clarity. For what did not serve you, that which you may term obstacles, deeply embedded from negative experience were released in one night in what could have taken lifetimes. The purging was appropriate in the first experience; it was what was required in your frequencal truth. Likewise in the second experience, there was teachers that you sought, and teachers that were appropriate in your expansion. Does that answer your query?

JT: *Yes, thank you.*

AA Metatron: *And so we continue in this most interesting discussion. We will tell you that the human experience is often riddled with adverse emotional reactions to life interactions, and certain restrictive energy obstacles occur in the emotional and mental bodies that close windows of the mind.*

Certain sacred plants of the psychoactive genre, when taken in ceremonial manner by a learned facilitator can assist in re-opening these doors and windows. Once opened, they rarely close again or remain open for a long time, and so quantum leaps in awareness and parity are enabled.

Yet, the plants that enable the hallucination of the mind can be most beneficial to some and less so to others. It is therefore imperative that one be able to navigate within perspective of the experience. That which you term illusion is in truth a corridor, a gateway of the mind that leads to other realities and dimensions.

For example, as we have said, the corridors opened by the medicine plant termed ayahuasca can lead one into unresolved embedded energies from traumas in the present and in other lifetimes by offering the path to the actual experience. In this way, the present or past life issue comes into clear focus, and the energies associated with it are relived in actual reality aspect with opportunity to release what needs be liberated to remove the trapped obstruction. One may also change the outcome or finish an uncompleted mission that was not completed in the previous experience. Accordingly, the mind is expanded to an array of multidimensional time hologram realities and is not locked into one perception. Many become available within what we call the focal dimension, the one dimension of Truth as it relates to the individual.

Preparation and Prerequisites

Yet be aware that strength and especially wisdom are necessary to accomplish these releases and completions. Simply having access to the doorway of expansion does not necessarily mean that one will have the key to open it or the ability to navigate within its offered realities. A certain level of intent, will, fortitude and light quotient are requisite to establish the conscious wisdom and ballast to navigate and manifest these benevolent outcomes.

Strength begets strength, and wisdom initiates even greater wisdom, but both require effort and preparation, you see. And it is essential to understand that one must enter these realms in a state of preparation and devoid of fear. For if one enters in a haphazard fashion, if one enters expanded reality states in fear, that fear must be overcome, or one will experience an amplification of that fear. Indeed, it is not an experience of frivolous pursuit.

Without these attributes, one merely hallucinates; one only experiences dreams and/or nightmares. And accordingly, one returns from whence they came without the rewards that were available. The vibration of the seeker must, then, match the highest purpose of the journey. Such plants were never intended for recreation, for entertainment, you see. One is meant to enter as if entering the holiest of Cathedrals, in reverence, respect and with great considered purpose.

If one enters the expanded reality realm without preparation, one will encounter an experience that has no redeeming merit. What one puts in, one will harvest. If nothing is sewn in sacred intent, nothing of value will be reaped. That is so in all endeavors of growth and of spirit. And with the highest intent, the ability to enter without fear is tantamount. That is among the preparation attributes required, for fear is ever the vibrational static of disruption, a frequency that is not harmonic to the experience, you see.

So let it be understood that there is indeed a sentient thought form of the highest order available within the experience of ayahuasca, which is presently by far the most profound of all the sacred plant medicines. It is the one, then, that offers the most gain and provides the highest frequency for wisdom. So if one misunderstands the purpose or misapplies the experience and enters haphazardly out of mere curiosity, the sentient frequency is not matched, and the greater experience simply cannot vibrationally occur.

Discernment

Appropriate application, optimal preparation is, then, requisite. And for that reason, Masters, they are NOT for everyone.

We will also add that while these plants offer an incredible opportunity for clearing and truth, they are certainly not the only method of obtaining such clarity. Yet it is an accelerated lens and one of great value when approached in preparation, readiness and proper frequency and light quotient. The plant carries an extremely high frequency and a great degree of the consciousness of the Earth itself, and accordingly it offers incredible transformation for those that choose this lens and for those that are ready.

Selection of Guidance

It must be said that the choice of whom is to facilitate, whom is to guide the ceremony is of utmost importance. Just as tedious preparation for the experience is essential, so, then, is the selection of whom will guide it. Such an experience must be facilitated by one of highest integrity, highest light and one with an appropriate affinity with what may be termed the conscious 'Spirit of the Plant.'

Closing

Divine dimensional light for each human is transmitted from within your own being, not from without. It is based upon the energy of one's own truth, the confirmations that are the Cosmos, and from that place they are aggregated. They are expanded within you as only light frequencies can be and then vibrate themselves into the mind and heart where, by the magic of your intent, they are converted to wisdom. But it is important that you will know that it is energy that you send, energy that you receive, energy that you speak and that you guide and that you call upon that reveals to you your true divine self. Points of light and infinity dot your planet, and they offer great acceleration. Lake Titicaca is among the most pristine of these. But the most important sacred site, you see, is within your heart, and you ever carry it with you. Such is the gift of the human kingdom on Earth.

I Am Metatron, and I share with you these Truths. You are Beloved.

And so it is... AA Metatron via James Tyberonn

James Tyberonn

Atlantis & Dr Moreau ~ The Metatronic Perspective on Yeti and Sasquatch
Archangel Metatron Channel via James Tyberonn

The below channeled information is excerpted from a fascinating Q & A session with Archangel Metatron via James Tyberonn. Pre reviewed questions on a wide array of topics, including Crypto-Zoology were posed for the 'channeled' interview.

Because of the format of the interview and the fact that this excepted section occurred in the middle of the text, the below extraction does not include the endearing opening and warm greetings of most Archangel Metatron channels. It is fascinating information and differs in many startling ways from what has previously been said by other information sources about these Beings. Discern & Enjoy!

Blessings, James Tyberonn

Question to Metatron: *You speak of the Earth having inhabited 'Hollow Chasms.' Do these subterranean inhabitants include the beings we refer to as Yeti and Devic?*

AA Metatron: *It does not. These beings also exist but are not among the LeMurians and early Atlanteans that ventured into the inner Earth.*

Question to Metatron: *Can you tell us about the Yeti, and are these the same as the beings called Bigfoot?*

AA Metatron: *These you refer to as Yeti or those termed Bigfoot are both mutations of earlier versions of the genetic experiments on Earth, primarily from the* *second phase of Atlantis, some 20,000 – 25,000 years ago in linear aspect.*

At that time, there were many genetic experiments on your planet. These beings are intelligent but genetically impaired. These massive forms were genetically created using human DNA with that of the ape to create a laboring humanoid beast, a beast with greater intelligence, human like intelligence but with imposed genetic wiring or implants that 'unplugged' certain areas of the brain.

These are survivors of those whom you term 'the others,' the genetic mutants of Atlantis. These are remnants of beings callously created for work force within mines, farms and forestry. The areas of their brains that allow for emotion and expansive thinking have been artificially impaired within their genetic codes. Yet it is the same source that inhabits these diminishing creatures that is within the dolphin, but within their bodies it is unable to find expression or mentally evolve beyond certain limits.

Yet they do possess that which is termed divine intelligence. But these beings are unable to effectively tap into the higher self because of the genetic disconnections. Only within their great physical endurance capacity, strength and survival instinct mechanisms are they able to sustain.

There are actually several 'versions' of these beings. The largest, most powerful and intelligent are those of the Himalayas, termed Yeti, and those of the Pacific Northwest and Siberia, termed Sasquatch or 'Bigfoot.' The 'version' of these mutant genetic experimentations that exists in the swamplands of the southern United States are smaller and less intelligent than the larger version of the Himalayas and Pacific Northwest. The ones referred to as 'Skunk Apes or

Swamp Apes' were a different primate DNA source combination.

These beings presently have a life expectancy of approximately 80 - 90 years. Less than 25 percent of the females are capable of reproduction, and the reproductive cycle is not annual. Populations are far fewer than you may imagine and are diminishing. There are less than 1,000 currently on the planet.

These beings do not live in the inner chasms of the Earth. They live in caves and remote mountains and within your deep forest and swamplands. They are nocturnal beings. They are a race that is dwindling, shall we say, and in time will no longer exist.

These beings have great wariness of humans, and experience a great dismay and confusion as to their evolvement. They cautiously watch you, they know they are your brothers and with baited anxiety want to be closer to you but are intelligent enough to know they cannot.

Their bodies have evolved to allow them, through the massing of thick hair and thick oily skins, to live in extreme locations. And here they live out their final era of life.

Their spirits no longer wish to complete, as their genetic limitations are such that they cannot evolve, yet they are entrapped in a cycle that is difficult to for them to emerge from because of the genetic limitations. The genetic filters or implants placed within their biology inhibits their ability to truly access their divine intelligence and so are sadly trapped in a recurring cycle.

If you were to look within the eyes of one of these beings, you would feel a great sadness.

Question to Metatron: *Are you saying that Yeti are the same spirit source as dolphins?*

AA Metatron: *Originally the same source, that being of Sirius, as are many of your species on the planet. But to be clear, whilst it is the same original source, it is not the same expression, in fact far from it. You see, these creatures cannot, do not express the same vivid emotion, intelligence and joy as do the dolphin, because the bodies in which they are entrapped does not allow them to.*

They are trapped incongruently between the matrix of 'group soul,' as is innate to that which is termed the animal kingdom, and individual divine consciousness enabled for the human and dolphin. They cannot access their higher self and as such operate in a dilemma between the two. Thus they are both attracted to and repulsed by both, in a manner of speaking, unable to fit in, unable to find expression.

The Yeti and Sasquatch were unsuccessful genetic experiments that entrapped life force, but unnaturally, inharmonically so. But because more primate DNA than human DNA were used, it was more successful, relative to the other horrific results. You see, this was done to humans as well in Atlantean (Aryan) experimentation. There were indeed semi covert genetic experimentation by the Aryans that literally created myriad abominations, not unlike your imagery in the 'Island of Doctor Moreau,' crossing humans with beasts of many types, birds, horses, bulls and primates, for untoward purpose.

Many parts of the 'fictional' Moreau tale are in fact somewhat similar to what occurred on Aryan. Drugs were frequently required to regulate the human side hormonally, and a form of remote shocks were used for behavioral control. In the mutations that were more human than animal, the relatively short existence was a horrid living nightmare ... an abomination.

With the Yeti-Sasquatch, the intent was to create a powerful creature capable of extremely heavy labor but to have no free will, to be remotely controllable, incapable of certain independent thought processes. You may wonder why such spirits would choose to inhabit such restricted physical vehicles, and the answer is that fewer and fewer choose to do so, and soon they will no longer exist as a species.

The ones remaining desperately wish to be out but have not as yet found the inner means to escape the entrapment. It may be said that they are enmeshed, trapped within the grid time gradient. But they are diminishing in numbers, because they no longer have the desire to procreate or the biology to allow normal birthing. In a few centuries they will be gone, totally extinct. These beings are capable of expressing great strength and natural animalistic cunning in survival and do have an undiffused innate kinship to one another, but they are quite aware in their greater aspects of their inability to expand in these corporeal expressions into their true nature and divinity.

Question to Metatron: *There are some who believe that the Yeti and Sasquatch are mystical beings and have a message for humanity. Based on what you have shared, is that inaccurate?*

AA Metatron: *It is inaccurate to assume that because they are enigmatic and mythical to you that they would be highly evolved.*

Very little of their true and greater nature can be brought forward. So in these bodies they are not enlightened beings, and while some humans in metaphysics may wish to think of them as evolved consciousness, with messages for humanity and abilities of invisibility, they truly are not. But there is a lesson learned.

These mutant beings have in many ways reverted back to an animalistic behavior pattern based on instinct. But they do not, cannot in the altered vibrational format, fit into natural patterns; and they are aware of this.

Their sleep cycles are yet capable of a fleeting connection to their Divine Mind, but in waking state it is absolutely blocked. For this reason, they sleep far more than they wake.

As stated , they are intelligent enough to realize that they do not fit, and they are conflicted by the desire to be a part of humankind and an appropriately wary caution of knowing what would occur if they are seen by man. As such, they will occasionally observe man from a distance or in close proximity camouflage ... with a vibration of curiosity and deep melancholy.

These beings are not aggressive, and stories of attacks are incorrect ... just as tales of communication with mankind are incorrect. Like large primates, they will when forced attempt to frighten an aggressor that invades their space, but unlike large primates they will not attack to hold their ground. While they live in small groups and nurture their young, there is no 'alpha male.' Instincts of dominance remain removed. They have no natural predators in their remote habitats. They are not carnivores.

Some have speculated that these beings are capable of becoming 'non-visible' at will. This is inaccurate. They do not flux between dimensions or disappear into parallel time frames. They do indeed have an extraordinary ability to camouflage themselves in the indigenous flora of their environ. They have learned how to blend. Once they detect human presence, they can remain silent and motionless as needed to avoid detection. Yet despite their enormity, they are capable of stealth and rapid movement.

These beings are nocturnal and have elaborated sleep patterns. Sleep cycles in dormancy occur on a 3:1 basis, approximately 30 hours of sleep/semi sleep for every 10-12 hours of waking activity. This is due in part to their inability to rhythmically flow with natural pattern and in part to escape their entrapment in dreamscape.

Because they were 'engineered' to be somewhat robotically controlled, certain of the sensory capacities were genetically amplified as a control mechanism. Their ability to perceive sound and vibration is well beyond that of any other land based mammal, including the canine.

You see, they were controlled by emissions of ultrasonic sound vibration by the Aryans. As a result of their enhanced vibratory senses, Sasquatch and Yeti have an ability to recognize the presence of humans by picking up the human brain wave from as far as two kilometers away. This ability is in the form of an enhanced telepathic sensory of thought and a high pitch sound sensory similar to the sonar of the dolphin.

Question to Metatron: *This feels very sad. Can we do anything to help them?*

AA Metatron: *Humanity in their genetic engineering via the Aryan Sons of Belial created abominations that were responsible for great misery. As we have said, the humanoid animals were horrific. The Law of One was aware of this and opposed to it. Not enough was done to halt it, and this (as well as the misuse of the Crystals) led to the sad demise, the downfall of Atlantis. The memory, and indeed the lesson, is ingrained deeply within the consciousness of the planet and the group mind of humanity.*

It is the pledge of the Law of One, to never allow these to occur again.

The past can be changed, for it is no more fixed than the future. There will be a resurfacing and leap in the technology of genetic engineering knowledge in the years to come. These mistakes cannot reoccur. That is how you help the remnants of 'Dr Moreau.' And, indeed, soon the Sasquatch and Yeti will escape the physical confines in the energies to come. Their chosen extinction is, in effect, in the crystalline energy of the Ascension that they cannot remain, will not remain.

You cannot, will not allow it to happen again, and in so doing you will erase the past. That is how you help them. By navigating the future that erases the past. Such is the maya of the purposed illusion of that which you call time on the University of Earth.

Dear Ones, just as the Law of One have pledged to never again allow the Crystals to be misused, there is indeed a pledge of equal dedication to not allow the genetic engineering to be enacted in abomination. It is part of the Ascension, it is your pledge. Do you understand? Then create it as so.

I Am Metatron, and I share with you these Truths.

And so it is... AA Metatron via James Tyberonn

James Tyberonn

Dancing With the Stars
Archangel Metatron Channel via James Tyberonn

Greetings, Beloved! *I am Metatron, Lord of Light, and I greet you one and all, respectfully and knowingly. I greet each of you individually within the exact moment in which you read these living words in the vibratory essence of the eternal NOW. I embrace you in love.*

As the heralded Ascension draws nigh, all around you is opening. The nature of your divine Starseed is expanded into Earth realms, indeed you are dancing with the Stars. The Stars of hope, love and impeccability.

Dear Ones, we of the Angelic Realm are here to support you, to offer insights of guidance, but it is up to each of you in sojourns of polarity and duality to master your challenges. These are your avenue of learning, and it is incumbent for each of you to face and solve your problems. We assist you by putting you in touch with your own power. Our purpose is not to solve them for you or to come between you and your own freedom of discernment and choice by giving you 'answers' even to the most complex of challenges.

Our purpose is to reinforce your own strength, for ultimately the vast divinity of your Being is not only well equipped to help you find fulfillment but totally desirous of doing so. And, Dear Human, in this process you will discover your higher nature of wisdom, understanding, exuberance and peace. No one, not even an Angel can do this for you. In impeccability you will achieve every self designed task before you.

Beloved, we offer in this moment the integral energy of our Light Beingness, of that crystalline essence of which we are. We offer you in pure love the guidance of our wisdom for your discernment. Masters, we ask of you simply to be fully present in your hearts and minds. Discern what we say, for you are a God in process. Take what resonates of that which we offer, for it is presented to you in deepest respect and love.

Star Dancing ~ Expanding in Love

The star dance of your life is to expand in love. But the love we speak of is not merely the emotion that you humans tend to think of as love. But rather the extraordinary magnificent energy and science of what may be termed expansive unconditional love. In this context love is indeed a science, a vast field that is composed of a very complex vibrational resonance.

So let us further define a key component of love resonance as it relates to your growth ... and that is the impeccability of actuated divine will. Will, as translated into action, is the driver of your search for spiritual growth. Impeccability, then, is the distillation of your present experiences and knowledge into the wisdom of action.

Accepting the Challenge

While it is true that your thoughts and beliefs create the reality you experience in duality, you in higher aspect thoughtfully and carefully compose and create the challenges that you face. These have great purpose. Whether you truly believe it or not, you write your own tests. So while 'positive thinking' is a key frequency, positive thinking is meant to help you approach your life lessons and does not circumvent the learning process itself. You cannot just ignore or wish away the growth lessons you script for yourself in order to expand. That is because your chosen setups are in most cases outside, beyond the ability of the duality aspect of ego-brain to remove or will away. You will face them, because you have, in divine self, willed it from higher perspective. In higher mind you have scripted your challenges.

We assure you that there is nothing more stimulating, more worthy of actualization than your manifested desire to evolve, to change for the better. That is indeed each of your lifetime missions. It is not enough to meditate or to visualize the desired goal being accomplished if you do not act upon the inner voice, the drive from which your meditations and visualizations arise.

Intent, focus and meditation must absolutely be teamed with action. Becoming impeccable and eventually achieving your enlightenment does not mean, as some religions indirectly imply, that you are suddenly in a blissful state of oblivion or in some distant state of nirvana. Masters, we tell you that you are as much a part of a nirvana now as you ever will be, you simply need to discover it within you.

There will indeed be cycles within your emotional state; that is part of being human. There will be times in which you feel apathetic and depressed. Not only the problems you face but even certain astronomical gravities can be the source of such despair on their own. All of these must be faced, and can be surmounted.

So be aware that 'Nirvana,' in your vernacular, is achieved attitudinally, not through avoidance, ignorance or escape but through impeccable confrontation of the reality projection that surrounds you. Earth experience, duality mastery is difficult. This is a great truth, one of the greatest truths of duality and one commonly misunderstood. The study and mastery of life requires work. You cannot simply put the text book under your pillow and sleep on it. It must be read and understood a page at a time, moment by moment.

So, then, your full understanding and accepting that your life is a construction of 'setups' that you planned in order to enable your spiritual growth is an even greater truth. You see, when you accept this noble truth, you have the opportunity to transcend it.

That which you term 'destiny' is in truth the situations you preplanned for your life lesson. And, Dear Ones, that very self scripted 'destiny,' in your terms, will assist you to both face your challenges and then manifest your desires but not because you protest what you do not like. In order to experience the light of your desire, you must ignite the passion that will free it from the stronghold where it has been closely guarded. The greatest path is to accept the challenge of self purification by being a living example of your own light rather than protesting the darkness that still exists within the world in 3-D or choosing to insulate yourself from it.

Acceptance

Masters, by accepting that you are here to face challenges, then you can more robustly create the energy needed to face them. Because once it is accepted, the fact that life can be difficult no longer scares you, rather it motivates the spiritual warrior into resolve.

The greatest issue you have in accepting ultimate ownership and responsibility for your actions lies in the core desire to avoid the pain of the consequences of that behavior. But we tell you that it is the confrontational courage of impeccably solving problems that provides and indeed nurtures meaningful growth in your life.

Facing your problems is the serendipitous cutting edge that distinguishes between success and failure or, better said, between growth and stagnation. Problems call forth your best effort to resolve and refine courage and wisdom within the impeccable seeker.

It is categorically because of stressful predicaments and obstructions that you grow mentally and spiritually. It is through the pain of confronting and resolving life puzzles and 'setups' that you learn the greater meaning of the science of love. Dear Hearts, the candid fact is that some of your most poignant accomplishments and indeed greatest growths are spawned when you are placed in the troubling crossroads of conundrum.

Your greatest trials and revelations take place in times when you are outside of your 'comfort zone,' feeing bewildered, unfulfilled or even in a state of agonizing despair. For it is in such moments, propelled by your discomfort, that you are compelled to burst out of the confining cages and seek a better more spiritually satisfying way of life.

Impeccability ~ The State of Grace

*What, then, is impeccability? We are not understating the base premise when we define impeccability simply as **'always trying your best.'** To remain impeccable requires more effort as the scope of your gained wisdom and consciousness expands. The greater your consciousness, the more you 'know.' The more you know, the greater the responsibility to live accordingly.*

You are in the process of expanding your vibratory awareness, of becoming a conscious participant with the soul. You are becoming what your soul is, discovering your greater identity. Dear Ones, when you grow spiritually, it is because you have opened to seek growth and are taking action, working to achieve it.

Impeccability involves the deliberate extension of your Beingness into evolution. Impeccability puts you in the state of grace. Impeccability does not infer that you have achieved enlightenment or have learned all you need to learn. Rather it means that you are on the only track, the right pathway to get there.

So we will define Impeccability in two layers, two phase formats:

1. ***Conditional Impeccability***: *This is when the entity is not highly advanced yet working toward Mastery. Doing one's best. Utilizing knowledge to the best of one's ability to do the right thing, even when there may be ignorance and innocent misconceptions. By that we mean you truly believe what you are doing is the right course, even if it is not the full or expansive truth. All of you go through such phases. In this phase if you make a mistake, it is an honest mistake in which you genuinely believed you were doing what you felt is right.*
2. ***Mastery Impeccability***: *This is the phase of the soul in human existence that is on the cusp of Mastery. One highly advanced and walking the talk. Having no inner conflict between what one believes to be the right path and what one actuates.*

Both phases activate that which you may term as an accelerated state of grace. Grace is assistance from the Divine Self to help the outcome of situations when one is trying their best. It may be thought of as the 'Guardian Angel,' because in many cases that is exactly what a Guardian Angel is, your Divine Self serendipitously intervening in situations to assist you on your path.

If we were to redefine what your religious texts consider as sin, it would not be in terms of the commandments, rather it would be: "knowledge not utilized." Taking actions you know to be incorrect, actions in conflict to your highest beliefs.

Wisdom Is Within

All of you desire wisdom greater than your own. Seek and you will find, and, Masters, you can find it 'hidden' inside you. And, sadly, that is often the last place you look. It takes work. You see, the divine interface between God and man is within that which your academics term as the subconscious.

Even your religious texts tell you that God is within you, that you are a spark of the Divine. The subconscious mind or 'back brain,' in your terms, is the part of you that is God. The portion of your greater self that contains the knowledge of 'All That Is,' the part of you that contains the Akashic Records, the soul memory of everything.

Since the subconscious is the Divine Mind within you, the goal of spiritual growth is achieved by entering into that sacred 'Garden of Wisdom.' It is entered by quieting the ego-mind. Meditation has ever been the gateway. It is the key to quieting the personality-ego narration and allowing the 'Voice of the Divine Soul' to be heard. We say again, effort is required. There are no short cuts.

The reattainment of God-ness is the purpose of your individual existence on the polarity plane. You are born that you might become, as a conscious individual, a physical expression of God. A divine expression in Beingness.

The challenge is your soul quest, your true purpose, and in physical sojourns the clock is ever ticking. Obtaining Godhood in physicality is achieved on time release, through immaculate desire that is actuated in the physical realm by merging with the wisdom of the non physical. Time matters.

In polarity, the current shifting of paradigms and energies can throw you off center rather easily in these quickening times. Your true purpose is often difficult to subjectively define, and your understanding and ballast lies juxtaposed between illusion and perceived reality. You may feel you are living in a distortion and that nothing is exactly as it seems. In the process, you can become confused and complacent. You can lose track of time.

Dear Ones, your lives, each moment of your physical life is precious, far more so than some of you realize. Far more than most of you utilize. Time is a precious commodity, and it is finite within your duality. Each of you reading these words will at some point in the future transition out of the physical. In your vernacular, you will experience death, you will die. This is a condition of physicality as you know it. Yet, so many of you act as though you will live forever. Indeed, the soul is eternal, but you will not ever be the same person, the same personality or expression that you are now, in any lifetime or in any other aspect of your 'Beingness.'

You are here to learn, Dear Ones, you are here to learn the expressions of your own Godliness within duality, and indeed duality is a gift. Life is a gift. You are here to learn how to cocreate, for indeed you are cocreators of the Universe, of the Cosmos. You are here to achieve Mastery, and so many of you are very close, very near that achievement.

Seize the Day

Masters, until you truly value yourself, you will not be in the grace of impeccability and thus not be motivated to truly value and optimize your time. Unless you place great value on your allotted time, you will not do your 'best' with it. "Carpe Diem" is translated as "Seize the Day," and this is so appropriate.

You must seize each moment! So many of you, despite your good intentions, allow yourselves to be tranquilized into complacency during certain phases or within certain conditions of your chosen sojourns. Many of you waste time; misuse time, and lifetime after lifetime can be squandered. That which you do not face, that which you do not resolve in any one moment or lifetime will resurface. You will repeat the setup until you successfully solve it, and that is indeed a great truth.

Masters, utilizing your time in duality is quintessential, and that is a complex undertaking, for it necessitates that you seek impeccability. It requisites love of self, for until you genuinely value yourself, you truly do not value your life and time. And until you value your time, you will not be compelled to maximize how you spend it.

Self discipline is necessary to accomplish this. Discipline contains the basic set of tools to solve life problems. Without discipline it is difficult for you to have the driver required to focus on the work of solving your problems. Simply stated, you can become immobilized ... apathetic, complacent or lazy. On the 'Ladder of Ascension,' you are either moving up, sitting still or moving down.

In third dimensional physics, there is a law that states that energy which is highly organized will naturally degrade when not in dynamic state. It is easier by natural law to be in a state of complacency in the physical plane than to be in an upwardly mobile condition. That is clearly logical. It is the Law of Love that motivates all souls into greater consciousness, and that requires dynamics ... work! Laziness is in a real sense one of your biggest obstacles, because work means swimming against the tide. Seize the Day!

Perfect Order

Some of you say and feel that, "Everything works out as it should, all is in perfect order." But, Masters, that concept is something of a paradox, and, like a face card, it is upside down either way you look at it. Do you understand?

From the higher perspective, all is in perfect order, but from the perspective of humankind within duality, it is not! If it were, there would be no need for lessons, no need for that which you term reincarnation.

One need but take a look around to know that the plight of humankind on the planet Earth is far from being perfect. Indeed, it will NOT work out as it should until you make it so!

This applies in micro and in macro. There is much to manage, much to review. All in time, and, Masters, it will occur. We herewith offer some of the lingering, more difficult issues for your contemplative review and discernment.

Hidden Ego ~ Spiritual One-Upmanship

Many of you are leaders and teachers and have worked long and hard to acquire an advanced level of knowledge and spiritual truths. This is admirable. But it leads to a crossroad of decision.

A human on the path of Mastery must avoid the pious trappings of self righteous ego, or you will be humbled in cause and effect. A leader must ever honor the soul-voice and follow their internally directed path in order to ascend rather than fall.

James Tyberonn

This is an essential compass for all on the advanced course of Mastery. Without inner 'soul review' and calibration, one cannot see the true direction home.

Understand, then, that with continued advancement comes the need for humility. How many of you have attended metaphysical gatherings only to be somewhat put off by someone who make it a point to let you know how far they travel in their dreams, how many great visions and celestial teachers they see in the higher realms? The implication being that they are advanced in mastery and want to be sure everyone knows it. Often the approach is in the guise of unsolicited assistance, with the overt trapping of letting the other know how special, how advanced they are.

This is an understandable pitfall but is not the true walk of integrity Spiritual 'One-Upmanship' is rampant in New Age circles, yet most offenders would not even be aware they are coming across in such a pompous manner. There are many covert trappings of ego within spiritual circles. No one is exempt. Leaders and teachers who advance to a certain level are particularly susceptible to this trapping of ego when they begin to achieve a following. Most that have it don't recognize it. Are you one of these? It happens to most at some point, Dear Ones. Humility is the way of the true spiritual leader, yet it is so easy to blindly fall into self aggrandizement and to place yourself on a pedestal to impress others. It is hard to recognize and even harder yet to admit.

We tell you in love, Dear Ones, that it happens to all of you. It happens in all of your lifetimes, the move and shift day to day, in and out of integrity. Within duality, whether you are a teacher or a student (and all of you are both!) none of you are above it. And that is why it is necessary to recalibrate through the infinite mirror of truth, of self review within the detached observer within self. There is such a fine line between self love and ego. The paradox is that the former is a necessity of impeccability and the latter is a hindrance to it.

On the path of Mastery you will be forced many times to choose between love and power, and power is very seductive and often well disguised. Pride comes before the fall. Many have risen to great heights in spiritual achievement only to lose it all by becoming blinded by ego.

There are two forms of power. One is used for control, political power, the other is true power, the benevolent power of Love. But as you progress in your awareness, you will find the distinction of power less a case of good and evil and more a case between love and deceptive concepts of power. It is about more subtle energies. There are energies that desire one movement or direction, and there are energies that would necessitate a different and more refined understanding. The challenge remains in putting all the pieces together, and this is not an easy task.

Sexual Integrity

True love is a frequency. It is not emotional passion, it is not romance and it is not sexual, in your terms. Above duality, in your true essence you are androgynous, integral, whole and non gendered. Only in the polarity plane of the physical realm does gender orientation occur. In your present time and plane of existence, the physical drive for sexual fertilization is within the current DNA model to preserve the survival of the species. This is neither needed nor present in your higher self, above duality.

Sexuality is another area that is very complex, very confusing for many of you. It is an area that requires impeccability.

Throughout the eons of time, there have been many systems of belief, many varied expressions, experiments and modalities within the various cultures across the planet on sexual expression within biology. Some were very inhibited, others extremely liberal. The deeper bonds of biological and spiritual love lie at the basis of all personal and cultural relationships, but there is a higher love that transcends well above your cultural and religious programming of sexuality.

Religion and culturally expressed morality standards in your present paradigm influence a great deal of oppression in terms of sexual expression. The resulting overly specific sexual orientation, then, reflects a firm division in consciousness. It not only separates the male from the more nurturing emotional impulses but also can separate the female from her own freedoms to project strength and intellect. It effectively formulates a restrictive culture in which mind and heart, strength and nurturing are divorced into polarity via gender.

Intimacy and sexual expression are vehicles for expressing nonphysical energy in physical ways. Sexuality can be sacred, or it can be mere lust. When it is a spiritual expression of physicalized soul union, it is experienced as far more than a physical act and is done from higher chakra intent and manifestation. In this instance, the vital life energy expended is amplified, sanctified and returned to the energy field of the participants and increases their vitality and balance. Each records the soul imprint of the other.

This is however, not the case when it is expressed on physical urge alone for the sole purpose of sexual gratification. When sexuality is enacted purely for physical hungers, the vital energy is simply expended, spent and is not returned to the human energy field. Indeed it some cases, the act when based on selfishness and gratification alone, leaves the electromagnetic field somewhat ruptured, and energy bleed can occur.

Most humans in your present society have conflicted issues around their sexuality and sexual expression. Sexuality is a format that can merge two souls into blissful unity as one, but it can also express one as One. It is the qualitative aspect of the participants' intent that determines the level of specific chakric flow, whether or not it is done in highest elucidation, you see. It is not ironic that many of you will achieve the highest balance in your lives only after your body ceases to produce sexual hormones.

Yet the release of kundalini, of chi through the sexual act is among the most powerful energies available to mankind. It has been used for good and has fallen into wasteful misappropriation. The key is intent.

When there is consensual attraction teamed with caring and mutual respect, it can be exquisitely sensual, beautiful and sacred. It is capable of transporting the spirit to higher realms, companioning the trinity of body, mind and soul.

Sexuality is the natural expression of love that flowers between souls. It can be the highest natural expression of love between people, regardless of gender. Yet it can become a source of guilt, a source of control and a source of bias and judgment. It can become a source of self aggrandizement and addiction, particularly among those of the male gender, because the male drive to reproduction is hardwired, so to speak, in the corporeal. As such, it is often misunderstood and even more often misused.

Relationships should be based on agreement, and the freedom of this expression should be honored yet optimally aligned

153

with the higher chakras. Dominance of one over the other is not congruent with true love in relationships of any nature.

High intent within sexuality is extremely beneficial on all levels, physical, mental and spiritual. It can be a source of rejuvenation and regeneration. Yet some choose sexual expressions that border on debauchery, manipulation, greed, self aggrandizement, conquest and a depletive addiction to physical orgasm.

Without judgment, we tell you that sexual energy is a gift of sublime exquisite energy that should be used wisely. When used in higher intent, it offers a sublime glimpse into the sacred orgasmic bliss of the celestial realms. It is embellished vital life force and should be enacted with discernment, intelligently and sagely, encompassing the highest merging potentials of body, mind and spirit.

When sexual expression is duly chosen, it is responsible enactment with highest intent, through heart sharing and love as an aspect of crystalline impeccability.

Unresolved Energy Blockage

Masters, on the final walk of Mastery, most of your major issues have been dealt with, and we honor you for that. What remains may however be elusive to confront. And it is important to confront any and all unresolved issues and energies.

We say this without judgment; we point this out in order to assist you. For in time all must be dealt with. The more advanced you become, the more difficult it can be to sweep up the last remaining bits of unresolved issues, because they are often well hidden. The unresolved energy, the final issues can become polarized and repelled outside your mental field, forgotten in the residues of many lifetimes. Dear Hearts, take time to closely self review in multidimensional, Mer-Ka-Na aspect. Please determine what is left to be worked on.

Polarity Physics

Masters, the closer you get to light, the stronger you attract the dark. Light attracts bugs! The more you advance, the more criticism you will draw, and that requires wisdom to deal with.

The polarity aspect of the 'Law of Opposite Attraction' herewith comes into play. From a state of detachment what takes place is electromagnetic. Pure positive energy has the greatest 'magnetic' attraction to negative energy. So as your light shines brighter, the magnetic force between polar opposites increases. It can be managed, but you must have the light, humility, the strength and discipline to appropriately deflect it and not to become entangled in the process and fall into a downward spiral.

So dealing with affronts, the hard energy of jealousy, hatred and anger are an important piece of the puzzle in achieving the Master level of Impeccability. How do you deal with this? Don't take anything personally is perhaps easier said than done, but it is quite true. Your bible talks of turning the other cheek. But to be clear, this does not mean that you apologize when someone steps on your foot. Part of the paradox is, indeed, standing up for your truth. But it does mean that you don't step on the feet of others, intentionally or otherwise. Do you understand?

Standing in your truth is peaceful action. It is a benevolent expression of aggression that allows grace and dignity to be retained on both sides of any conflict or attack. It sends the attacking energy back to its source but without malice and with love.

Each of you has an opportunity to stand in impeccability within any conflict. You can deal with conflict without exacerbating engagement. Do you understand? Deal with the situation by facing it head on from a stance of emotional detachment as the observer. And that is not easy, yet it is the way of the Master. It is how you 'Don't take anything personally,' you detach from any entangling emotional reaction.

Each of you has an opportunity to be impeccable every day. The scenario in which you recognize your own failings, your own conflict with integrity is the day you encompass Mastery level Impeccability, and indeed it is a journey. Likewise, the day you stand in your truth with willingness to recognize another person's truth, you encompass integrity.

The divine mind is only achieved, only accessed through crystalline Mer-Ka-Na resonance within crystalline thought waves. Crystalline thought is above emotion, above petty feelings. It is achieved in detachment. It is the crystalline lake of Shamballa, of true Nirvana, as smooth as glass, no waves distorting its mirrored visage.

Closing

In closing, we offer our blessings and gratitude for your seeking. What is more precious than your life and its divine purpose?

Your role now and tomorrow is ever to seek fulfillment, understanding and impeccable unfoldment. Your divine mission can and will create a beautiful merging of purposeful experiential reality ... of dancing in joyous starlight and projecting the rays of that crystalline beauty to all around you.

There is no ecstasy more supreme than achieving the Divine mind. It is why you are here. You are of the realm of Creatorship, of Mastery, and you are far closer to its physical manifestation than you know. Dear Ones, YOU created the Ascension, and it is dawning now. We honor you. The heralded time you have dreamed of awaits you, Dear Ones.

I Am Metatron, and you are beloved.

And so it is... AA Metatron via James Tyberonn

James Tyberonn

The 2012 Express ~ New Earth Demands of 2013
Archangel Metatron Channel via James Tyberonn

Greetings, Masters! *Indeed! We greet you in joy and encircle each of you in a field of Unconditional Love.*

Masters, 2012 is not an end, rather it is the true Beginning. Accordingly, December 21, 2012 is the initial point of the expansion of dimensional access on the New Earth. Accordingly, the New Earth truly begins in 2013, and a dynamic acceleration extends and amplifies exponentially over the next four decades.

The Ascension has movement. It does not occur in one flash. It's progression after the winter solstice of 2012 is likened unto that of a train moving downhill.

Momentum is gaining force! Energies of the Earth are shifting more quickly now. The velocity of light has increased. In response, the flash and sequencing of linear time is moving faster now, in the quickening of the 2012 Ascension. The magnetic grid is being reduced as the Crystalline Grid becomes dominant. Gravity fields have transitioned and will continue this process. The arc swing of duality is lessened, and the movement into greater dimension, crystalline frequency is now tangible. It effects you and influences your Beingness in a powerful manner during the shift.

New Earth Demands

In kind, then, does the need for humanity to shift become requisite to maintain equilibrium and balance. Equivocation will not serve. The astrological undulations become more intense as does the heightened energy of the planet itself.

The energy of the New Earth demands more effort on your part. You must proactively raise your frequency to adjust, to keep pace. You must manage expectation and rise to the occasion.

The new energy is of a different medium. Just as you move differently in water than on land, so must you adjust your energy field in the new expanded environ. A new focus is necessary in the optimal maintenance of your Auric Body, for the human EMF (Electro-Magnetic Field) is being shifted into CEF (Crysto-Electric Field) at the level of the 5th dimension. It is an important change and is a mandate for each of you on the path.

Ascension Symptoms

The Ascension has symptoms. How you choose to deal with them has consequences. They become either growing pains that lead to great new horizons or the impetus of a stagnation that can lead to a downward spiral. You cannot sit on the fence and ignore it; one of the two, the former or latter will occur. The Ascension energies are global and are encountered through Auric Induction. The Aura must be understood and maintained in order to shift into the Crystalline. The higher frequencial energies of the New Earth require a larger CEF (Crysto-Electric Field), and the operation manual is a bit more complex.

If you do not make a concerted effort, the greater resonance will create fissure cracks in the field, and you will have energy bleed. Energy bleed creates short circuitry and leads to greater malfunction including potential symptoms of depression, anxiety, chronic sleep disorder and apathy. These can be avoided, but the mechanics must be recognized and monitored. It is more important than ever to understand and, indeed, rigorously maintain the Auric Field in the ongoing shift, for it is the optimal CEF that is the gateway to the Crystalline Light Body.

James Tyberonn

2012 Requires Beacons

Yes, it takes work to adjust. But it is the better path. It will, at times, seem overwhelming. But you can navigate this with discipline and heart. And we are here to assist.

The greatest path is to accept the challenge of Self Ascension by being a living 'Light House Beacon'. Project, then, the example of your own light, rather than protesting the darkness that still exists within the world in 3-D and choosing to dimly insulate yourself from it. Not all humans will chose the walk of Ascension at this time. In many ways it is a moot point, for the changes of the Ascension will occur whether or not humanity, in micro or macro, shifts in synergetic rhythm in sync with the New Earth of 2012. Beloveds, we offer in this moment the integral energy of our Light Beingness, of that crystalline essence of which we are.

We offer you in pure love the guidance of our wisdom for your discernment. Masters, we ask of you simply to be fully present in your hearts and minds. Discern what we say, for you are a God in process. Take what resonates of that which we offer, for it is presented to you in deepest respect and love.

Our purpose is ever to reinforce your own strength, for ultimately the vast divinity of your Being is not only well equipped to help you find fulfillment but totally desirous of doing so. And, Dear Human, in this process you will discover your higher nature of wisdom, understanding, exuberance and peace. No one, not even an Angel, can do this for you. In impeccable Mer-Ka-Na you will achieve every self designed task before you.

2012 Optimal Auric Circuitry

And so we speak on the optimal circuitry of the human auric field, with specific focus on the 13-20-33 circuitry. Masters, the

Human Aura is not autoregulated. It requires methodical maintenance. And this is tantamount, because achieving and retaining the 13-20-33 Circuitry of the integral Auric Field is an absolute prerequisite of ascending into the Crystalline Light-Body Vehicle. You see, with the great expansion of the resonant energy via the completion of the Crystalline Grid, it is logical to understand that a crystalline light body is generated and birthed in order to carry the higher crystal energy matrix of the Ascending Earth. It is the Mer-Ka-Na, and its circuitry is an Alchemical process that must be understood in order to operate in optimal quantum clarity.

Auric Development

Now, we address briefly the linear time aspect of development of the Human Aura. Dear Ones, as each of you have grown in consciousness through your multitudinous sojourns in duality, you activated more layers of your auric field. With each new activation, more responsibility is required, greater perception is naturally requisite for optimal Auric maintenance. The ultimate and optimal resonance is the Circuitry of 13-20-33. This is the key ratio and flow of the graduated, fully blossomed Auric Field. It is this resonance that allows for flow into Crystalline Light Body. Unless the 13-20-33 is obtained, cultivated and sustained, Light Body acquisition is untenable.

Before we delve into this important essay, let us add the caveat that Auric expansion is a journey and not a destination. In other words, what is gained MUST be kept. Many of you have achieved high levels of Auric layer activation, only to lose the clear luminosity and circuitry due to lack of comprehension of the fundamental stipulations required for optimal Auric Field sustenance.

James Tyberonn

Most of you whom are termed 'Old-Souls,' in your vernacular, originally entered the Earthplane in Crystalline Light Body, in the Mer-Ka-Na of the true Ascended Master. With the Fall of the Firmament, you willingly entered into the 'University of Duality' and in time lost the connection to the great and greater aspect of your true essence. Your auras then took a downward spiral alongside your awareness as you fell into the diffused density of polarity physical bodies. This we have shared with you in earlier essays.

Now we wish to clarify at this juncture that the advent of duality onto the Earthplane was not an accident. It was what we may term as a deliberate occurrence to allow for the experience and growth within duality. The Earth became a University in its role as the Planet of Choice. Most of your religious scripts refer to this as the 'downfall' of mankind. But in actuality it was an intentional 'maya,' an illusion with purpose. Duality placed filters on consciousness, and work was/is required to 'grow' back into full crystalline consciousness. But ALL of YOU chose this growth, and it carries succinct credentials.

The duality experiment carried with it certain vulnerabilities and allowed for, what may be termed, purposeful setbacks. This, then, is the journey of duality, the contractual pathway for reemergence through growth and overcoming of obstacles. And so, in this process of re-growth, the dense became denser, the physical became more solidified and the hemispheres of the human brain became locked in the polarity of the dodecahedronal grid.

The duality cycled human, then, incarnated into lifetimes that were dominated by frontal mind and the experience of lower chakras. This level of unconsciousness then allowed for only the 7 layer chakric field, with the goal of activating from the lower 3 chakras to the upper 4 in unifying the seven in full flow.

Duality was defined by polar electromagnetics, and the grid system that determined the level of density was the magnetic or gravity grid. This was indeed adjusted to differing levels throughout the progression of humanity. For a great deal of the linear time since the Golden Age of Atlantis, the gravity grid only allowed for an 8-8-16 circuitry in the Human Aura, and the gendered Mer-Ka-Bah was the Light Body that enabled growth from this level of frequency. Certain Avatars came back into duality from 5,000 to 2,000 years as you measure 'back' in linear time from this succinct reality hologram, in order to begin to reestablish the pattern resonance of 13-20-33.

Yet, only from the Harmonic Convergence of 1987 did the grid adjustment truly rebirth the 13-20-33 potential for the masses. This became initially enabled with the 144-Crystal Grid in 2001. It is the Crystalline Age through the Crystalline Grid that fully empowers the return to 13-20-33 upshift into the reemerging Crystalline, non polarity Mer-Ka-Na Tri System.

Circuitry ~ The 13-20-33

The 13-20-33 is an energetic emulsion interface combing the connectivity between antimatter / matter / etheric matter in a crystoelectric amalgam that creates the energy hum of OM. As such, the circuitry of 13-20-33 is not only the optimal frequencial flow required for complete cosmic auric function and upshift, it is the only frequency that can do so. It is the key, and a complex one, that serves as the 'plug-in' for full power. Indeed, it is then and only then capable of carrying immense energy. It untangles and combines variegated heterogeneous and homogenous energy forms in a compatible unified matrix that is capable of flowing into zero point, Crystalline Field of Mer-Ka-Na.

This circuitry implements and administers the mandatory linkage between the 33 components of the integral field. It is, in fact, the junctured manifold that regulates the appropriate networking resonance and lattice weave within and without. It is defined as follows: the 13 represents the 12 layers of the Auric Field within etheric matter harmonized and synchronized into Oneness. Thus, the 12 becomes the One forming the 12 + 1 = 13 frequency. It only occurs after sufficient sojourns in duality allow the consciousness of the entity to activate all 12 layers and tie and activate the 12 primary chakras to each layer of the aura and, indeed, to the 12 strand DNA.

The 20 represents activation of human auric interface layers into multidimensionality within the realms of Antimatter. These layers were not easily accessible until the adjustment of the magnetic grid occurred.

The Fibonacci synchronization of the 13 + the 20 enables the 33 circuitry. This enables the circuitry that allows for humanity to expand fully into the Crystalline, non polarity levels of consciousness. This is truly the vehicle that takes you full circle, full circuit ... back home.

The Mechanics of Maintenance

Now, the correct flow of the 13-20-33 circuitry is dependent on certain maintenance responsibilities as we have described. We will discuss now the obstacles that are most common in obtaining and sustaining optimal circuitry.

Issues Effecting Auric Integrity:

- *Opposing Energy Fields*
- *Emotional Stress*

- *Conflict*
- *Planetary Energy Expansion*
- *Negative Thought Form Attachment*
- *Air Travel – Physical Overstress*
- *Medications, Alcohol Excess, Toxins*
- *Inappropriate Attitude / Control Issues / Ego Imbalance*

Some of these are herewith addressed in detail.

EM Fields and Microwaves ~ Biopolar Reversal

In your current times, the electromagnetics of the ascending Earth are being amplified in potent surges, pressurized surges that can stretch and microfracture the flow and symmetry of your auric fields. This is a fundamental and defining necessity of the Ascension, as you morph into expanded 13-20-33 Circuitry Auras in order to achieve 3rd level Mer-Ka-Na within the Mer-Ka-Na Tri System.

In your age and usage of cell phones, computers, televisions and electronic devices, your offices and homes are in constant barrage of opposing electromagnetic energy fields. The result can be a temporary 'short circuit' effect that, if unresolved, can lead to auric imbalance by means of energy loss through fissure cracks. In essence, this may be termed 'auric bleeding.' Some of the effects are short termed, but others can become chronic.

The detrimental effects of electromagnetic fields and microwaves, from microwave ovens, computers, mobile phones and televisions have been recognized by some of your mainstream medical professionals. These tend to be minimized and ignored by the masses, in part because the very suppliers and manufacturers of these generators of microwaves and magnetic fields sponsor and underwrite studies from staff or consulted scientists and *'experts' with the pre-contracted aim of disproving or vastly minimizing the contra effects. In fact, the detrimental effects are very real, and most of you are constantly within these contra fields. As a case in point, most of you will read this message in front of a computer screen.*

Dear Ones, there are effective methods of dealing with these contra fields. And these will be offered to you.

But do not ignore the fact that these fields will absolutely have varying levels of negative effect on your auric field. Most of the in situ waves and fields do not penetrate very deeply into the layers of your auric sheath. Others do, yet all can fissure your energy fields. There may be some who consider this to be an issue of belief system or that this very message to be one of fear. It is neither. It is true that an Ascended Master can transmute such effects, but, Dear Ones, we tell you in love that unless you are manifesting at that level and can walk on water, take heed. The detrimental consequences of microwaves and electromagnetic waves created from alternating currents are a succinct certitude for the masses of humanity in duality, whether you believe it or not.

While these effects are not life threatening, they do indeed affect your energy circuitry and can create that which is termed 'reverse biopolarity' and auric short circuitry. Both of which can lead to auric fissuring and result in auric bleeding.

Air Travel

Air travel is an ingrained aspect of most of your lives. At some point almost all of you will travel by airplane to another destination. And such travel depletes the aura far more than is currently understood. Indeed, expansive regular air travel can shorten one's very longevity and cut short life span, especially for those in mid to later years. Pan continental and trans ocean flights by the very measure of their copious distance and requisite time in flight are exponentially more degenerative to the human auric field. Virtually everyone aboard a 9-10 hour international air flight exits the plane at their destination with varying degrees of irregular or ruptured auric function. Long distance flights traveling latitudinally in eastbound vectors are the most detrimental. Yet, all such take an undeniable toll on the energy field ... you call it jetlag. Such a benign term is a gross understatement, for the condition is far more than simple fatigue from time zone change.

Now, one of the key underlying factors at the root of the issue is that most commercial planes fly at altitudes of 35,000 feet, in the stratosphere, and effectively outside the regulatory pulse of the Schumann Resonance. The Schumann Resonance is the planet's 'heartbeat,' it is an anionic charge released by the Earth that combines with the cationic charges released from the stratosphere to form an electromagno capacitor around the planet from ground level up to about 30,000 feet. This capacitor forms a background resonance that plays a key role in regulating vital organs and glandular rhythms in the human body. Airplanes flying at 35,000 to 37,500 feet, as most do, are outside this regulatory range, and the metallic fuselage of the aircraft further deflects most remaining integration. The result is a distortion of the physical rhythms. Your NASA agencies and space station agencies are aware of this issue, as it has created chronic physical issues with the astronauts. They have experimented with placing magnetic generators in the stations and shuttles.

Your medical personnel that have studied jet fatigue are aware that flights can and do force the heart to work harder, and that longer range flights enlarge the heart temporarily. The pilots and flight attendants who fly daily absolutely stress their bodies and auric fields to the extent that chronic diseases result and 'aging' is acutely accelerated. There have been internal studies of the abbreviated life expectancy of airline flight workers, but these are for the most part kept from the public. They are indeed aware that hypobaric hypoxia caused by pressurization of the aircraft alters rhythmicity after long flights, independently of the number of time zones crossed and significantly reduces human hormone levels.

This issue is somewhat exacerbated by the rather cramped conditions of sitting in close quarter seating for extended periods in which rest is difficult, circulation is impaired and the body ingests less oxygen, resulting in a fatigue of its own. The extremely dry air in the pressurized cabin as well as the pressurization itself is detrimental. Cycles are interrupted, and indeed most of you recognize that it is difficult to rest the body after long flights. Insomnia occurs as but one side effect of the auric circuitry interruption.

Now let us be clear, flights of under 3-4 hours are not as detrimental as the 8-12 hour variety, and recovery is much faster. So other important factors include the time in the flight, the frequency of flights taken and the age and physical health of the individual human. Yet all flights, as we have emphasized are detrimental to varying levels.

Equatorial Crossing

Long flights of latitudinal crossings invoke greater fatigue to the body physical due to time zone change. This occurs in addition to all of the other factors mentioned. Yet, longitudinal flights that cross from the southern hemisphere to the northern hemisphere (and vice versa) invoke another frequencial adjustment to the auric energy. The resonant energy below the equator will, in unforced and unmagnetized scenarios, naturally rotate clockwise below the equator and counterclockwise above it. Thus, when one flies from below the equator to destinations above it, and vice versa, the individual's Auric circuitry will be negatively affected for a period of time.

Question to Metatron: *Many people have jobs that require flights. What can be done to minimize the detrimental effects?*

AA Metatron: *The effects, again, are exacerbated according to the frequency of flights and length of flights. Other factors are the general health and age of the person flying. So in all cases, try to minimize regularity and frequency when possible. Maintain the health in all activity. When you know you will fly, you can stabilize the field somewhat by wearing copper or gold on both wrists and by employing certain gemstones as rings and pendant to help hold the field intact. After the flight, take salt mineral baths and avoid sleep aids. Hydrate the body as much as possible during and after the flights.*

The Crucible of Ascension Magnetics

Other less obvious but vitally important sources of auric diffusion are the very mechanisms of the Ascension. This may seem paradoxical at first glance, but indeed it is occurring, and you must be aware of this. The primary mechanisms we refer to are the solar winds, the increase in the spin of the planetary core and the resulting amplification of planetary frequencies. The planetary pulse is speeding up, and, Dear Ones, it is affecting you in myriad ways. In a very valid sense, what is occurring through the ascension energies is stretching your frequencial capacities. As such, you are required to grow a new expanded auric field, much like a snake that annually outgrows its skin and goes through a phase of fitting into a new one that can better encompass the larger body. Do you understand? Before the new one can become resilient, the old one is stretched and cracked. And during that transition there is a phase of metamorphosis that encompasses within it certain vulnerabilities until the new one is completed.

As your Earth draws closer to the Ascension of 2012, many major changes are occurring around you that have a profound effect on your physical, emotional and mental well being. Many of you find that you become somewhat 'vulnerable,' feeling overwhelmed at times, as if you cannot seem to get things done, as if there are not enough hours in the day. Some of you are going though periods of depression; you feel as though you are sinking into a funk, and it seems like you are moving through molasses. Emotions go from ecstatic highs to deep lows shadowed in dark despair. Dear Ones, you are not alone. Literally millions of you are experiencing this stretching and building of the 'new auric skin.' And we say to you that by understanding the process and maintaining the integrity of your auric field, the process becomes much easier.

Case in Point

The channel has often spoken of an energetic equalization that can occur when seekers initially visit powerpoints or sacred sites. When a non resident seeker goes to a mega-powerpoint such as Mount Shasta, Lake Titicaca, Sedona, Arkansas or Glastonbury, for example, many find themselves enveloped in a much stronger resonant electromagnetic field than they are accustomed to, an energy much stronger than the resonant vibrational rate of their auric field. For some, but not all, within 3-7days, depending on the auric strength and resilience of the individual seeker's field, the auric ovid will stabilize the pressure differential in a form of osmotic equalization. The auric field will do this through the formation of tiny fissure cracks, and a rupture of the auric sheathing will naturally occur.

Unless the individual deals with it, an auric short circuitry eventuates, resulting in energy loss. Such emotional extremes can occur up until the time that the auric field is restabilized and regrounded.

For people that move their residence from lower energies into the locale of a mega-powersite, this process can take from six months to a year. Those of you who have moved to the Mount Shasta and Sedona areas will understand this. For visitors, it will correct itself within a week or two of going back to their place of residence. The key is to be aware of your auric frequencial quotient and to not overstay your time, until your field is capable of holding the higher frequency.

Now, we are not saying that it is not beneficial to visit powernodes, quite the contrary. Such expansion in the overview is inevitable, quite beneficial and quite necessary in order to grow the 'new skin' required to expand into greater frequency and multidimensionality.

Powernodes accelerate this process and as such should be visited. These infinity points are virtual accelerators that aid your metamorphosis and prepare you for the heightened energies of the ascension, you see?

Rather, we are saying that there are processes occurring within powernodes that are a microcosm of the macrocosm, and that they need to be understood. You see, your entire planet is beginning to quicken, to increase in frequency, and you must ready yourselves to contain that frequency. Many of you are dealing with this somewhat in the dark. You are now or will soon experience this, and an understanding of the process will serve to make it much easier.

Auric Metamorphosis ~ Changing the Etheric Skin

The reverse process is also occurring within many of the more enlightened souls. There are many of you who are already tapping into your expansive multidimensionality, as the 144-Crystalline grid enables greater dimensional access. The result is that your inner Crystoelectric Field is pulling in great surges of energy, energy levels that are somewhat greater than the parameters of your auric capacitors. In these cases, the result is that a stretching, an overload occurs resulting in temporary fissure cracks and energy loss. You are changing your skin.

Part of this metamorphic stretching requires a cleansing process. The very multidimensionality of powernodes and of the Ascension itself are 'crucibles' and will force one's issues to the surface and thus allow the entity an important opportunity to confront and release any imbedded obstacles. Better sooner than later. This is why these are popping up for so many of you. Attempts to rebury them, ignore them will simply cause the issue to grow and fester. These issues themselves, unresolved, will generate stress and lead to the reactive fields of polar reversal, circuitry failure and auric bleeding.

Dear Ones, truly there is a metascience around auric integrity. This is not a new science, rather a forgotten transitioning one. But one that must be understood, relearned by all who seek to grow, all who seek balance, wisdom and knowledge.

An intact auric field allows one to rebuild the Cosmic Lattice and achieve 13-20-33 circuitry and, as such, multidimensional *expansion through the levels of the crystalline Mer-Ka-Na system. A fractured field loses energy, and the energy loss stresses the physical circuitry. If the loss is not recognized and reconciled, it can lead to chronic polarity reversal, emotional lows, depression, chronic fatigue syndrome, insomnia, migraines, weight gain, anxiety and panic disorders, to list but a few. These can be reconciled.*

Now, we encourage all of you to actively study this subject. What you must understand, however, is that there are many diverse sources of detrimental EMF impacts that can slow the 'metamorphosis,' creating varying degrees of temporary circuitry damage to the field. And these must be dealt with. Imagine these as slow leaks to the tires on your vehicle. If ignored, the tire will go flat, and the vehicle cannot move forward. So it is with your auric field.

Question to Metatron: *How does one recognize auric bleeding?*

AA Metatron: *First by understanding certain conditions that can create energetic imbalances and auric energetic diffusion. Those we have listed in the above discourse. The human Aura has certain built in defenses. Just as your skin has three levels of sheathing, so to speak, your auric fields have twelve layers on the Earth dimensions. The outer three levels are where most of the energetic diffusion takes place from electromagnetic waves; microwaves can affect you on much deeper levels.*

Microwaved food reverses the molecular polarity of the food substance being heated. This is a recognized fact within some of your mainstream academia. When this is taken into the body, circuitry within the digestive system and bowels are affected, both in the physical and energetic bodies.

Now, the precondition recognition is essential, first by knowing within which situations auric interference from opposing energy fields can occur. Sensory indications can be quite subtle. The first sensory indicators are emotional lows, a sense of being tired and out of sorts. Humans rarely connect this to Auric energy loss, because it occurs quite commonly due to the fact that most homes contain interfering fields. And the course of life within families, jobs and daily life have their stressful aspects. Aspects that are indeed in part due to energy loss from the taut hectic pace and worsened by lack of exercise and healthy diet.

Question to Metatron: *What can be done to strengthen and solidify the Human Crystoelectric Field?*

AA Metatron: *There are many things that can strengthen the field. But first, try to eliminate the root source of auric short circuitry and diffusion. Stop using microwaves for food. If it is a case of being obliged to spend hours in front of a computer, as many of you do, there are steps that can be taken to neutralize the bombardment.*

Now, exercises to strengthen the auric field are numerous. Some of these are conventional methods, others are not.

- *Exercise at least 30 minutes per day (Tai Chi, Yoga or Walking)*
- *Increase water consumption, and magnetize water*
- *Detoxify through saunas, colonic irrigation, massage therapy*
- *Use salt baths, mineral baths and thermal natural springs*
- *Utilize the Tesla Violet Ray Therapy*
- *Use of magnetics on the soles of the feet and wrists (<3500 Gauss)*
- *Wear specific combinations of gemstones*

- *Wear noble metal around the neck and on both wrists*
- *Healthy diet*
- *Avoid excesses of alcohol*
- *Elimination / minimize toxins, tobacco and certain prescription drugs*
- *Take cleansers weekly such as raw garlic, ginger and cider vinegar*
- *Work with Phi cut Vogel crystals in auric sealing*
- *Smudge, sage the field*
- *Utilize pure sonic frequency through crystal bowls, Tibetan bowls and tuning forks*

Now, in addition to this, be aware of your emotional state. If you are suffering from lethargy, chronic fatigue, insomnia, depression and anxiety, it will certainly serve you to take the steps listed above, but other actions will likely be required. Many of you have chosen certain life lessons that involve removal of obstacles by overcoming 'contractual setups.' These setup life lessons are in essence opportunities, gifts if you will, to allow you to move forward. If they were easy, you would not necessarily learn. Simply changing your outlook to 'positive thinking' when you are dealing with a life lesson that leaves you in a state of lethargic depression is not enough. A 'Pollyanna' outlook will not resolve the core issue. Nevertheless, an intact auric field will assist in overcoming these issues, and in certain cases the auric field will not be whole until these chronic issues are resolved. One provokes the other and vice versa.

While some of you may be somewhat 'karma free,' most of you still have learning to walk through and issues to clear. The current time is a gestalt to allow you to achieve these lessons and to confront and remove remaining energy-viral obstructions. Auric maintenance underpins all.

Question to Metatron: *Can you advise if the 'neutralizing* *chips' that are available to eliminate detrimental effects from monitors and computers are functionally valid?*

AA Metatron: *Except for the individual's degree of 'belief,' they are currently of very little assistance beyond the 'placebo effect.' At the present the 'biochip' technology is not of a sufficient advancement to be truly effective in its own merit. The most beneficial means to deflect these fields is fivefold, the first point being applicable in all conditions of field strengthening to negate interference:*

1. *The wearing of gemstones is far more helpful than the current neutralizing chips. A single refractive gem of 2 carats or more worn on one hand and a double refractive gem on the other hand helps deflect the fields. Examples of single refractive gems are diamond, garnet and spinel. Double refractive are aquamarine, sapphire, ruby, emerald, tourmaline, topaz or any of the quartz varieties such as amethyst, peridot and citrine. In reference to the double refractive, a carat size of 4 or greater is better. Combine this with noble metals on each wrist; gold, palladium or platinum is best. Silver, copper, brass, titanium and carbon steel will assist if the more noble metals are not affordable. Wear a chain around the neck with a stabilizing pendant such as lapis lazuli, malachite or azurite. Through this process you have a greater ability to increase your field and deflect opposing ones, you see. Clear gems are great producers of higher dimensional light waves, amplify one's field and help hold it intact. Do not wear beryl (emerald, morganite, alexandrite, aquamarine) and corundum (ruby and sapphire) at the same time.*
2. *Try to maintain a distance from the screens. For computer monitors this is difficult; for televisions, 4 to 5 meters is recommended.*

3. *Placement of ionic generators, such as halite salt blocks and air filters are beneficial in restoring the anion to cation ratio in rooms that contain computers, microwaves and televisions.*
4. *Utilize the Tesla coil violet ray and light beam applications with noble gases to balance the field and correct reverse polarity conditions and to assist in sealing the field from auric bleeding.*
5. *An efficient neutralizer of the effects of a computer is the placement of an iron nickel meteorite on one periphery of the screen with a block of malachite on the other. Each of these should be at least one pound in weight.*

Question to Metatron: *Some metaphysicians and shamanic teachings speak of 'psychic attacks' occurring when the auric field is 'open.' Can and does this occur?*

AA Metatron: *It can and does, indeed. However, your term of psychic attack is in truth an aspect of electromagnetics and harmonic oscillation. From a higher perspective, these are part of the setup and overlay of growth in duality, as you learn to be responsible with your innate creative forces. As we have told you, your thoughts and emotions have a vibratory frequency within duality that is quite real and quite alive. When you focus on an event or react in strong emotion to another person or situation, you create energies termed thought forms. These amass harmonically in various manners. If you project great charges of emotionally charged energy such as anger, jealousy or love, passion and joy toward another, you will agree that both parties are affected, yes? If you consciously dwell on these charged vibratory thoughts, then the energy mass, normally short lived, can gain sufficient momentum to become an aware thought form. When spiritual love and compassion are projected and created, a synergy occurs that befits both parties. When fury and hateful* *negativity are projected, a toxic reaction can occur from both sides. If the auric field of the 'targeted' person is open, the effect is worsened somewhat, and a temporary energy bleed can result.*

Now, it is important to differentiate between malicious or controlling energies and honest reactions. If someone disrespects you, the appropriate honest reaction can be one of pure anger and hurt. When these are openly and honestly expressed, a cleansing gestalt occurs that can lead to better understandings and a renewed, improved communication. It is a learning process and is appropriate. But nonetheless, a form of energetic opposition takes place.

However, when one person feels a vendetta or a prolonged desire to control the other, the gestalt can dissolve into charged conflict, and as such a malicious energy battle of will may occur. Very often both parties feel 'right,' and the frequency of hate harmonically attracts more and more like energy until the amassed energy form is so potent that it has the ability to effect a destructive 'attack' role to both. Unless one or both sees the wisdom of releasing the hate, it will pull them into a downward spiral, creating dis-ease and deeper negativity.

When one is in a state of malicious anger or self loathing depression, that vibratory resonance on its own will deplete and open the auric field. It becomes a self dug pit that gets deeper and deeper. Lifetimes can be wasted. Yet on a higher perspective, much learning occurs. There are times when great souls choose life lessons of overcoming such energies. Some evolved souls such as Gandhi and Nelson Mandela chose setups to be wrongly accused and convicted of crimes and to spend years in the negative energy of your prisons to learn to find peace and strength of will under the harshest conditions of oppression.

Now, when you are in conflict, insure that your auric field is maintained, and do not allow yourself to fall into malicious reaction. It is not wrong to react in honesty, but the narrow path of mastery, is to not fall into hatred and malicious revenge. You see, getting caught in these traps is much easier than getting out of them. Hate attracts more hate. When groups oppose one another, the collective of like thought forms amass, blend and oppose one another in enormous conflict. Very often entire warring nations form collective energy fields and reincarnate in these groups to continue these conflicts until it is finally resolved. Your current Gulf Wars are such an example, a rollover of the Crusades. Your World War II was a continuation of the Atlantean conflicts between those of Poseida (Law of One) and Aryan, (Sons of Belial).

Double Edge of Thought Forms

Very often, the most difficult 'attacks' are due to one's own negative thought forms coming home to roost. Perhaps the most difficult of these is around learning self love. When one falls into depression, self rejection or self loathing, the attack is self generating. The thought forms these dear souls create can become so potent that the auric field splits into personality fragments. A figure eight pattern of negative energy is emitted, amassing and flowing back through the opening of the solar plexus. The thought form of self hatred achieves a certain level of independent awareness and will become a very real obstacle, a self imposed dungeon until the person learns to face the root of the problem through great effort of will and wisdom.

Energy exchanges occur quite often in daily life. Some are mutually beneficial, others are not. It is important to note that energy cannot be taken from one whose aura is intact.

Healers constantly give energy within an intact aura and are essentially unaffected by the transfer. As such, love energy is passed from higher sources, and the healer's auric field is capable of willingly being the conduit without losing any of his or her auric field energy. But take note, if the healer is not in 13-20-33, circuitry healing cannot be truly provided. In fact the opposite can occur, a scenario in which both the healer and the one to be healed both lose energy.

Control and Energy Projections

Now, anytime you feel anger at someone, those thoughts are projected. Anytime someone tries to control you or vice versa, an energy projection is launched. There are, of course, situations in which it is appropriate to follow another's direction. You do this in every aspect of your life; it occurs in offices, the military, in schools and between children and parents.

This is based upon agreement and is properly germane when not abused. However, it is not befitting in these and other circumstances for one to allow another to abusively dominate their spirit or to maliciously attempt to break their will. Abuse of power often occurs in relationships, marriages, in work, in the family and social scenarios. In certain scenarios, as described, it is wrong to allow another to abusively impose their will, and it is equally wrong for one to seek such control outside the appropriate structures of agreement. This can evolve into a form of, in your terms, 'psychic attack.' The controller attaches to the solar plexus center of the controlled party and literally takes their energy, interjecting a destructive domination. This 'vampiring effect,' in your vernacular, especially occurs among egocentric people, controllers and manipulators. It often is attempted unconsciously by people in imbalance and depression who need a 'lift' from being around others due to their own energy shortage. It also takes place on a larger scale in patriarchal dogmatic religions, male dominated societies and in marriages. It is more difficult to counter in such trappings. When one is aware of being the target of malicious energy projections, auric integrity is of vital importance.

The visualization of enveloping 'white light' is the generally accepted protective mechanism. However if the auric field is open, the light visualization is not enough. The procedures listed to strengthen and seal the field listed above should be utilized. Be aware that anytime you have strong emotions of a negative nature or you dwell in depression, your fields will temporarily fissure. These attacks can only be energetically depletive if the field is open. The projected negative energy is easily repelled when the auric field is wholly intact. In such 'wholeness,' the energy is reflected back to its source for the sender to deal with. There is a lesson here, and Dear Ones, do not be the sender of malicious energy. Inevitably it will come back and cause you great remorse. Such is the nature of the law of harmonic oscillation.

Religions are often the source of great inappropriate control, control through fear. Even within the 'New Age,' in your terms, have sprung up gurus and spiritual teachers whose fame and power leads to the downward spiral of ego, self aggrandizement and control. The path of leadership and power inevitably forks, and one may be blindly tempted to take the path of greed and power over love. It is part of the lesson, and many have fallen into such traps of ego. When this occurs, they become 'energy takers.' That is why you should never blindly follow any leader or channel. Rather use discernment, and attune to your own Divinity. When you become a part of any 'group consciousness' and then decide to break free, there is a natural pull from the collective to bring you back in. And, as such, a form of 'energy attack,' in your vernacular occurs,

James Tyberonn

especially in possessive collectives who work at recruitment of followers.

Question to Metatron: *You mentioned combinations of specific gems for strengthening the auric field. Can you elaborate on this?*

AA Metatron: *This topic is a vast one and a book on its own. Briefly, gemstones, relative to auric maintenance and strengthening, are in essence benevolent conscious generators of force fields that reinforce and fortify one's own EMF. Being crystalline in matrix, they also are tuning forks that assist in 13-20-33 Auric Circuitry and, indeed, in Mer-Ka-Na formation and expansion.*

A basic combination would be to wear a single refractive stone, such as diamond, garnet or spinel, on one hand and a double refractive stone on the other. The best single refractive is the diamond, but it needs optimally to be a solitary of at least 2 carats, and we realize these are price restrictive. The best substitutes are garnets, preferably the Ural Mountain green demantoid or a red orange spessartite. Both project the octahedron in crystalline form. The diamond projects the dodecahedron and octahedron. If one can afford it, a combination of colors among single refractives is best. These can be intuitively alternated according to astrological forces and one's cycles. Garnets come in virtually all colors except blue. The spinel comes in pink, red, blue and violet.

In terms of double refractive gems for rings, the most potent are emerald, ruby, sapphire, morganite and aquamarine which project the largest fields, assuming a 3-5 carat size. Alternate colors as cycles shift. Tourmaline, topaz and quartz varieties such as opal, amethyst and citrine are all piezoelectric and also quite potent force generators.

Gem use is not folklore, indeed they are crystalline force field generators of crystalline coherent light. They can increase one's vitality and even prolong life span, particularly when used in tandem. You would do well to study this topic. Remember the body is bi-symmetrical, hemispheric. Combine gems with metals about both wrists and the neck. Noble metals such as gold and platinum are most potent. Silver is tertiary but quite benevolent in its aspect. Alternate these. A pendant about the neck is also recommended. Study this topic, and live it.

Closing

The process of achieving and maintaining crystalline clarity in the energy of higher dimension is a sacred process which the ancients understood in the Divine Art of Alchemy. Many of you are now making quantum leaps, but in order to maintain the integrity of the gains, it is essential to comprehend the basics and walk in impeccability.

Even the reconnection, Masters, to your own (past life) sojourns of higher development requires focal dedication and work in this lifetime. There are many pitfalls, and imbalance can create delusion if the process is short circuited. There are no short cuts to impeccability. It is why the true seeker on the path of Mastery never asks, "How much more work is required?" That is because Mastery is a journey not a destination.

You see, the best teachers are students of the eternally expanding process, and the self calibration of personal review is ever a tool in their medicine kit. The basics are never laid aside, never forgotten, never outgrown.

Dear Ones, the pace of change is quickening on the path of the Ascension. Change, as you are learning, is the Nature of All

Realities. You must now realize that the transition of the Auric Field is a requisite for holding great and greater energy and to evolving into Crystalline Light Body Mer-Ka-Na through the Metatronic Keys. The Circuitry of 13-20-33 is a profound step on your way to greater reality and Divinity Consciousness.

I Am Metatron, and I share with you these Truths. You are beloved.

And so it is... AA Metatron via James Tyberonn

About James Tyberonn

James Tyberonn worked as a professional engineer and geologist for 33 years. He is a native of Arkansas but has lived and worked abroad for over 30 years, circumnavigating the globe many times and traveling to over 75 countries in his geology work. Tyb has always had a very deep love for the Earth and a driven interest in spirituality and metaphysics all of his life. During his 33 years of working abroad, he devoted himself to intense metaphysical studies in varied disciplines. He focused on understanding the energy of the living Earth from both a scientific and a metaphysical perspective.

Tyberonn has recently been a featured guest speaker at the United Nations S.E.A.T. in New York City in late August of 2011.

A military veteran, Tyb served his country as an officer in the US Army Signal Corps. In his geological work, he lived as an expatriate in Bolivia, Brazil, India, Venezuela, Gabon, Congo, Russia, United Arab Emirates and Scotland. He studied gemology while in Brazil and speaks Spanish, Portuguese and French. He has had a great interest in metaphysics, sacred sites, grids, ley lines, portals, vortexes, healing gems, crystals, auric maintenance, Crystalline Light Body, spiritual growth and music.

As a musician, he produced and recorded a music CD of blues and jazz. All of the proceeds from the CD are donated to charity, the Foundation for the Cure of Cystic Fibrosis.

Tyb is a member of the Sierra Club and a staunch environmentalist. He has a great love for the planet and believes the Earth to be the living sentience of GAIA. He has visited over 300 sacred sites across the globe during the past four decades. He has been a guest speaker at the 'Elders Speak' Conference in Sedona, Arizona and at the 2007 Eagle and Condor Elders Gathering in Peru, attended by

James Tyberonn

over 100 Native Americans including Spiritual Head of the Mayan Nation, Don Alejandro Olax. He has hosted many Earth-Keeper conferences and pilgrimages to sacred sites. Tyb has been a guest on numerous metaphysical radio programs including *The New Earth*, *Voice America*, *Awakening Now*, *News for the Soul*, *VOA*, *BBC*, *Infinity Radio*, *Souls in Transition*, and *Mystical World*.

Tyb has mixed Native American heritage and has completed seven 5-day prayer fast vision quests in the Lakota modality, as well as several 3 1/2 day fasting dance ceremonies. He has had numerous shamanic journeys in Mexico and in South America. He currently resides in Texas. He has authored four books, cowritten a fifth with Lee Carroll (*Kryon*) and Tom Kenyon (*The Hathors*) and is currently writing his sixth book on the metaphysical healing properties of gemstones.

Tyberonn began channeling Archangel Metatron in 2007 and is featured each month in the *Sedona Journal of Emergence* magazine. He retired from his geological work in mid 2009 and now writes and conducts seminars and sacred site travel throughout the globe on a full time basis.

His extensive travels and time as an expatriate allowed him great opportunities to learn other languages and cultures. He is truly a "Citizen of the World" and dedicates his life to sharing the spiritual and sacred scientific information received from Archangel Metatron.

> *"I am a Citizen of the World,*
> *and my Nationality is Goodwill."*
> **Socrates**

Website: wwww.Earth-Keeper.com
Email: Tyberonn@Earth-Keeper.com

Other Books by James Tyberonn

"The Alchemy of Ascension" paperback

James Tyberonn's third book is a brilliant compilation of cutting edge channels from Archangel Metatron. Topics include the new Crystalline Light Body with in depth discussion of requisite Auric Maintenance and the geometry of the new tri system Mer-Ka-Na. The new light body correlates to the Crystalline Transition of the planet and the 144-Crystalline Grid, which will be in place for 2012. Several chapters focus on the new Crystalline Light Body processes and tri levels of development (Mer-Ki-Va-8; Mer-Ka-Va-12 and Mer-Ka-Na-20). Other topics include the Increasing Spin of Planet Earth, Earth Changes, 13-20-33 Auric Circuitry, The Polarity of Power and Love, Divine Sovereignty, The Crysto-Electric Cosmos & Antimatter and the Angelic Realm. This is a fascinating 'must read' for the serious seeker and metaphysician.

"Earth-Keeper Chronicles: METATRON SPEAKS" paperback

Read the inspiring and amazing channels of Archangel Metatron on: Planetary Grids, Reshel Grids, Vogel Phi Crystals, The Fall of Atlantis, Atlantean Master Crystals, MerKaBah and Mer-Ki-Va, Ley Lines, Sacred Sites, Sacred Waters, Healing Gems, Auric Maintenance, UFOs, Sasquatch, LeMuria, Hollow Earth, the Eagle and Condor, Earth Changes, Time Travel, Multidimensionality, Nonlinear Time, Reincarnation, Black Holes, White Holes, The Cosmic Trigger, Global Warming, Hologramic Dimensional Inserts and the Flashing Nature of the Universe.

James Tyberonn

"Earth-Keeper: The Energy & Geometry of Sacred Sites" paperback

The Cosmos, our Universe and our Earth are composed of living conscious energy ... the conscious energy of geometric light and electromagnetics. Our Earth is multidimensional, and so are we. Twelve dimensions exist upon our planet; 356 dimensions reside in our Universe. Geometry, sacred geometry is the mosaic underpinning of them all. Our planet contains a three in one grid complex that encompasses the Earth. This grid system enables and facilitates our experience on the planet and the fabric of reality in which we live. In specific places on our planet, these grids are unified into concentric vortex-portal templates and allow for all 12 dimensions to occur in a more tangible manner within a concentrated area, which I refer to as zipped space or harmonic dimensional overlay. When we as humankind enter into these special areas, we become immediately affected. One's energy increases, one's awareness is enhanced and one's multidimensional aspects are more tangible.

Books available from www.Earth-Keeper.com

Other Media Offerings from James Tyberonn

MK-3: "Metatronic Keys Level III" DVD Set

The Metatronic Keys Level Three: Mer-Ka-Na – Opening 33 Chakras in Crystalline Light Body, Establishing Conscious Creation.

The MK-3 DVD Set contains a live Archangel Metatron channel and a recording of the Metatronic Keys Level Three course taught before a live seminar audience. Included is an Auric Purity Meditation, lectures on Auric Maintenance, Mer-Ka-Na mechanics, function, responsibilities and the meditative process of installing the 3rd level of the amazing multidimensional Crystalline Light Body, the Mer-Ka-Na.

MK-1 & 2: "The Metatronic Keys Levels I and II" 5 Disk Set

The Metatronic Keys Level One: Mer-Ki-Va – Auric Mechanics and Maintenance, Establishing 13-20-33 Circuitry as a requisite of Mer-Ka-Na Field.

The Metatronic Keys Level Two: Mer-Ka-Va – Changing the Past, Releasing Final Obstacles, Harmonizing the Multi-dimensional Lifetimes.

5 Disk Set: One audio Meditation CD and 4 DVDs of the Mer-Ki-Va and Mer-Ka-Va, Levels I and II Courses. Complete with 33 page printable PDF of Course Material.

MK-1: "Mer-Ki-Va Installation Level I" audio Meditation MP3 download

James Tyberonn

The Metatronic Keys Level One: Mer-Ki-Va – Auric Mechanics and Maintenance, Establishing 13-20-33 Circuitry as a requisite of Mer-Ka-Na Field.

"Energy Giving Back – Blues for Cystic Fibrosis" music CD (100% of sales go to the Foundation for Cystic Fibrosis)

Songs Included: All Along the Watchtower, Bring It On Home, One Way Out, Can't You See, Wilde Mountain Thyme, Knockin' On Heaven's Door, Tangerine, Summertime, For What It's Worth, Voodoo Child, Hootchie Cootchie Man, Norwegian Wood, Tyberonn Shuffle, Moonlight in Vermont, The Tree that Never Bends, Trouble in Mind Blues, Stormy Monday, Rock Me Baby, Blue Bossa, People Get Ready.

Musicians: The Tracey Lynn Band, Lady D and the Blue Flames, Cachd au Craddoch Celtic, Dave Wilde Band, Darcie Deauville, Marvin Dykhuis, Chip Dolan, Tha Lady D, Little Stanley, James Tipton, Wally 'Mr Slide' Gator, Mark 'The Sax' Aston, Roddy Munro, Lindsey Frasier, Nigel Seaford.

Recorded in Findhorn, Scotland and Houston, Texas
Producer and Musical Director: James Tipton
Executive Producer: Bryan Dudman, *Help Find the Cure*

Media available from www.Earth-Keeper.com

Online Courses from Earth-Keeper

"The Alchemy of Ascension" Earth-Keeper Webinar Course
6-Month Study with 2 Webinars per month

A new look at ancient wisdom with cutting edge revelations in the shift to the Crystalline Age within the Ascension. Taught in two levels, including: Multidimensionality, Meditations and Visions, Dimensional Travel, Shamanic Path, Medicine Plants, The Law of Attraction – When it Works and Why It Doesn't, Inner Earth, Remembering Atlantis, Creating Abundance, Sacred Geometry, Grids and Grid Systems, Ley Lines, Vortexes and Portals, Sacred Sites, Simultaneous Time and Time Holograms, Parallel Dimensions, Crystals and Healing Gems, Extraterrestrial Life, Black Holes / White Holes / Matter / Antimatter, The Flashing Nature of Reality Consciousness, Phi Crystals.

> *"Change is the nature of reality, but certain laws remain ever in place."*
>
> AA Metatron

"The Metatronic Keys" Saturday-Sunday Webinars by Earth-Keeper
Given in two parts over 2 days

The Ascension Energies, Auric Maintenance, Preparation and the 8 Point Crystalline Mer-Ki-Va, The Earth is Transitioning to Crystalline Energies via the 144-Crystalline Grid. The Crystalline Light Body Tri System Mer-Ki-Va*Mer-Ka-Va* Mer-Ka-Na are the new light bodies that begin in the Crystalline Phase of the 5th Dimension and Expand to the 12th. The Earth is transitioning

James Tyberonn

to Crystalline Energy in the Ongoing Ascension Expansion ... Are You?

The Metatronic Keys Level One: *"Auric Maintenance, Preparation and The 8 Point Mer-Ki-Va"*
The Metatronic Keys Level Two: *"Multidimensionality and The 12 Point Mer-Ki-Va"*
The Metatronic Keys Level Three: *"Mer-Ka-Na Mastery"*
The Metatronic Keys Level Four: *"Teaching Certification"*

Register for online courses at www.Earth-Keeper.com